Reworking Retirement

A Practical Guide for Retirees
Returning to the Workplace

ALLYN I. FREEMAN AND ROBERT E. GORMAN

BUSINESS

Avon, Massachusetts

Published by Adams Business, an imprint of
Adams Media, an F+W Publications Company
57 Littlefield Street, Avon, MA 02322. U.S.A.
www.adamsmedia.com

ISBN-10: 1-59869-213-5
ISBN-13: 978-1-59869-213-6

Printed in the United States of America.

J I H G F E D C B A

Library of Congress Cataloging-in-Publication Data
is available from the publisher.

This publication is designed to provide accurate and authoritative information
with regard to the subject matter covered. It is sold with the understanding
that the publisher is not engaged in rendering legal, accounting, or other
professional advice. If legal advice or other expert assistance is required, the
services of a competent professional person should be sought.
—From a *Declaration of Principles* jointly adopted by a Committee of the
American Bar Association and a Committee of Publishers and Associations

Many of the designations used by manufacturers and sellers to distinguish
their product are claimed as trademarks. Where those designations appear in
this book and Adams Media was aware of a trademark claim, the designations
have been printed with initial capital letters.

This book is available at quantity discounts for bulk purchases.
For information, please call 1-800-289-0963.

Contents

Acknowledgments

Our writing on this vast topic owes much to the many people we interviewed. We sought out experts in academia, human resources professionals, administrators of volunteer organizations, and businesspeople. In addition, we tapped old friends from high school, college, and our neighborhoods for personal stories and anecdotes. Let's mention all those who were so helpful.

Professionals and Experts

William Brisk, Fellow of the National Academy of Elder Law Attorneys; Professor Marcie Pitt-Catsouphes at The Center on Aging and Work at Boston College; Josephine Smith; Lisa Mark; Kathleen Shelby; Bob Moore; Steven Berkenfeld; Carol Taffet; Martin Taffet; Mardee Cavallaro; Fran Panasci; Diane Brannen; Rick Consodine; Ernie DelMonico; Jack Crowley; Doug Fielding; Tom Pastorus; Ann Miller Patch; Patricia Dore, Angelo Sinisi; Paul Piccone; and Joe Frank.

Stories

Carrie Rosenthal, Bob Moore, Ernie DelMonico, Angelo Sinisi, Doug Fielding, Ann Miller Patch, Pat Holt Clarkson, David Moore, Gene Hicks, Gia Campos, Richard Lewis, Ann Driscoll, Tom Hetherington, Robert Greber, Harvey Stick, Mike Herman, Arthur Solomon, Jon Prusmack, Sam Marrone, John Hoffen, Jess Marlow, Julie Thacher Plummer, Karen Kolbert, Karen Goodman, Rudy Marzano, Rod McGarry, Royal Bruce Montgomery, Dave Poster, Ron Clifford, Rita Montequin, Dr. Dick Sebastian, Bob Wasky, Ed Wepprect, Finbarr Murphy, and Don Freedman.

Family and Friends

Dr. James Hunt, Ann Gorman, Rob and Laura Dingman, John and Linda Fullylove, Jason and Amy Weaver, Alison Gorman, Dick and Jane Erdtmann, Susan Faux Lewis, Cynthia Jenner, Janice Lee, Jeff Chase, Edward Last, Arthur Anderson, Charles Clarkson, Claudia Craig, Deb Green, William Rosenthal, Christine and Steven Rhodes, Marcia Shrock, Ruth Marzano, Maria Allende Brisk, Ella Kelley, Grace Anne Starkey, Steven Gross, Jane Monaghan Marrone, Pat Barry, Graham Graham, Margaret Intrator, Basil da Cano, and to the loving memory of Jo-Ann Wasserman.

Publishing

Also, many heartfelt thanks to Jill Alexander and Peter Archer at Adams Media, who vetted the project and were helpful throughout the process with suggestions and improvements. And to our agent, Ruth Mills, whose help and guidance crafted the work from beginning to end.

Introduction

"Live long and prosper."

—Mr. Spock

You are age fifty-five or sixty or sixty-five. Maybe you planned well for retirement. Maybe you did not. Or maybe you do not want to think about retirement because you believe that the word doesn't affect you today. Or maybe it does apply but you do not want to face that reality. Maybe you planned well for retirement but your company reneged on the promised pension. Or perhaps your company said no more medical benefits.

Or your plans worked out fine but retirement isn't the joy and delight you anticipated. Money seems to be flowing out. Time hangs heavy. What to do? You have a long life ahead. How are you going to pay for it—the food, the rent, the vacations, the medical bills? The everything? What plans outside of playing golf and bridge do you have to make every day more enjoyable and productive?

Will social security payments, which you can't start to take until age sixty-two, be enough? And Medicare doesn't kick in for you until age sixty-five. If you are fifty-five now and not working, what will you do until then to cover health insurance and medical payments? Perhaps you will run short of money to cover the necessities. Other than pension, savings, or social security, there are no other sources of income.

Perhaps you are bored out of your mind, and every day looks like the last one. Are you sleeping later and going to bed earlier to shorten a dreary day?

There's one terrific solution for people older than fifty: return to work or find new work.

Note that we did not say to get a full-time job, although that is an option, and we did not say to go out and find a new career. We're talking about remunerative jobs that you can work at about twenty or thirty hours a week—more time if you want to, more hours if you need to.

✔ It is easy, if you know how and what to look for.
✔ It is easy, if you know how to access information and facts.
✔ It is easy, if you do some short-term and long-term planning.
✔ It is easy, if you understand what it is you are looking for.

We know about looking for work, and we're going to share that information with you in this book. *ReWorking Retirement* is the definitive guide and one-stop resource for helping you overcome the difficult emotional and business-related obstacles of looking for and finding suitable and rewarding work.

We've made the book easy to read and easy to follow, with practical advice given in each chapter. This book should become your starting place on the vital topic of work because:

1. We are skilled professionals and knowledgeable businesspersons in our late sixties who have experienced firsthand the existing problems of finding and taking on new work assignments.
2. The chapters address the concerns of those people fifty and older who are attempting to search for work opportunities. The experienced advice inside the chapters offers you a real-world range of programs, lists, Web sites, and solutions.
3. The basic approach to work topics is practical and story-generated from numerous factual accounts of people like you who considered jobs that were in some way different from their earlier career. The real-world examples demonstrate the variety of things you can do to resolve work dilemmas, whether

you're seeking employment for income generation or for personal satisfaction.

Throughout the chapters we list key tips from experts. We asked post-fifty-year-old professionals to share useful and sensible suggestions based on their own experiences, concerning such matters as staying on the job, part-time versus full-time assignments, interviewing techniques, selling on the Internet, taking advantage of the retirement community, becoming an adjunct professor, retiring and working overseas, and many more.

Each chapter also contains stories of retirees who have parlayed previous work experience and/or hobbies into interesting post-retirement jobs.

The Appendix provides up-to-date listings of federal and state organizations to contact via e-mails, Web sites, telephone numbers, and street addresses.

The book's main goal is to make it easier for you to pursue work opportunities. Everyone who reads this book should "live long and prosper."

Robert Gorman
Winding River, NC

Allyn Freeman
New York, NY

1 Reality Check: The Facts

"Facts are precious things."

—Alfred P. Sloan Jr.

Demographics are shifting. In the United States people are turning age fifty at a rate of four million per year. Couple that with the number of people already older than fifty years of age, and you can see that the older segment of the population is expanding rapidly.

It would be short-sighted to believe that your plans for retirement and work will not be affected by the current swelling of the population. Everything from the gross national product to the cost-of-living index to the national savings rate, along with numerous other measures, will be influenced by what people your age do to stimulate or slow down the economy.

The Four Horsemen of the Retirement Apocalypse

In the biblical book of Revelation, the ominous Four Horsemen of the Apocalypse were called War, Famine, Pestilence, and Death. In that unwritten American book called Retirement or Growing Older, the Four Horsemen are called Longevity, Penury, Past Expectations, and Apprehensions.

We could add a fifth horseman: Fear of Being a Burden.

Longevity

It is a cheerless but basic economic fact that the longer you live, the more money you will need to pay for housing, food, medical, elder care, and other costs. Major medical advances are keeping people healthier. The result is that many more Americans are living longer.

An example of this longevity phenomenon: White males born in 1950 had at birth an average life expectancy of sixty-seven. When that population reaches sixty-five years old in 2015, these men will probably live an additional thirteen years to age seventy-eight. Couple the fact of living to age seventy-eight with the increasing number of births that occurred in 1950, and the result spells serious economic problems housing, feeding, and caring for this large number of septuagenarians if they do not have funds to pay for the prospect of a longer life. And who knows—by the year 2025, the age of men could increase another five or ten years.

The population statistics are startling. Every day, approximately 14,000 Americans turn fifty years old. Men and women born in 1957 represent the tail end of the explosive burst of births that began immediately after the end of World War II, the much mentioned and now clichéd "baby boomers." Some started to turn sixty years old in 2006, resulting in an upsurge in media stories.

The big question is: What will be the outcome of this ongoing increase in the nation's senior population?

In the near future, will social security benefits be fully funded to compensate this larger-sized, longer-living population segment that dutifully paid into the system during their lifetimes? Will Medicare funds be available to pay for medical care and drugs?

In addition, what about long-term care for an aging population, possibly depleted of income? It is a potential time bomb that could wipe out savings completely, especially when one spouse enters a nursing home and the remaining spouse must pay for the care. In this dire circumstance, the healthy spouse must exist on what is left over from retirement income. How will so many millions of seniors pay for the basic necessities of life? Living longer will be a blessing for some and a problem for others.

Penury

Call it penury, poverty, pennilessness—it's the condition of older Americans without sufficient income to pay for daily expenses. The two Ds, debt and divorce, have also been major factors in the adverse financial circumstances that affect seniors. Divorce doubles individual needs, requiring two households to replace the one family residence. The duplication of household payments, from rent or mortgages to all consumer needs from shampoo and soap to computers and televisions, may be a boon to the economy, but maintaining these payments and purchases necessitates additional income.

The major source of unwelcome debt for seniors comes from a habitual overspending on credit cards. Seniors, on average, carry monthly credit card balances greater than $30,000 (higher than the national average) and do not save adequate money for later years.

A couple in their late fifties ran up more than $100,000 in credit card charges for unforeseen medical procedures and stated, "To pay off this debt, we used up our meager savings, and both of us will have to work until we're dead." Their sad story is not a rare example. We all know other families that suffered similar catastrophic losses.

Even lifelong workers who projected retirement money from the company-funded pension plans may find out that these sources do not exist in the future or will be considerably less than anticipated. When this shortfall occurs, pensioners will suffer a significant loss of expected retirement funds that cannot be replaced easily, if at all.

In the 2005 United Airlines bankruptcy case, more than 120,000 employees were despondent when a judge ruled that the company could default on its pension obligations, which totaled $9.8 billion. Pilots experienced losses of up to 50 percent of their pensions.

The ReWorked Life

Investments to Ball Club Owner

Arthur Solomon grew up and attended high school in New Haven, Connecticut, went to college in Rhode Island, and eventually moved to Massachusetts. He retained a great affection for New England and was happy to develop real estate property throughout the region.

Before the move to Boston, he had been a partner in Lazard Frères Real Estate Investors in New York City, one of the most successful residential and commercial real estate organizations in the country. Solomon cashed out of the Lazard partnership and started DSF Real Estate Investors in Boston.

However, organized baseball seemed to be beckoning him from afar. His son had once been recruited by the Philadelphia Phillies organization, and his wife's father played baseball for one of the New York Yankees' minor league teams. Solomon started to look around for a potential minor league baseball acquisition.

Initially, he looked into the Boston Red Sox affiliate, but the Pawtucket Red Sox team—the PawSox (AAA) in the International League—was not for sale. Neither were the Portland, Maine, Sea Dogs (AA) or the Lowell, Massachusetts, Spinners (A).

In 2004, Solomon purchased the New Hampshire Fisher Cats in Manchester. The Double AA team had built a new stadium, seating close to 7,000.

Solomon is excited by the prospect of expanding the team's attendance and providing the highest quality family entertainment to the state of New Hampshire. From the air-conditioned owner's box, he can look down on a full house of happy New England families enjoying the national pastime.

When asked why he indulged in this purchase, he replied, "I did not want to be the wealthiest person in the cemetery."

What would you do if your company defaulted on its defined benefit pension plan, and no promised monies were available? The retirement income you counted on would disappear.

The question to ask is: How secure today is the company's defined benefit plan? One way to verify its status is to pay more attention to your annual statement, as it is required by law to indicate the financial security of the plan to employees.

For every person whose company or firm promised medical benefits for life, these perks are also quickly disappearing. Families that once thought they would not have to pay any medical costs now must pick up these medical insurance premiums at a hefty and ever-increasing cost.

Millions of senior citizens will have adequate savings, pensions, investments, and/or social security benefits to pay for life's expenses regardless of pension deficits or reduced medical benefits. But at least as many will likely have to find other sources of income to cover basic costs.

Statistics indicate that at age fifty, less than 75 percent of the population has banked even a paltry $5,000 for retirement. The "Buy now, worry about paying it later" mindset contributes to many seniors' naive attitudes that social security and equity from selling the house will fund the retirement years.

Many homeowners are delighted with the rising cost of houses and plan to bank this income to fund part of their retirement. But some homeowners have already dipped into home equity to buy luxury goods and other lifestyle purchases for consumption today. Families may take out home equity loans at a low interest rate, but they still must pay off this debt. In the drastic case of someone needing long-term health care, more equity from the house will be depleted to fund the new medical expense.

Another example of insufficient retirement funds comes from the nation's new Medicare drug program. Many fixed-income seniors suddenly learned that they could no longer cover some or all of their medications under the new plan with its difficult-to-understand "doughnut" payment drug system.

And who in their current retirement projected the vast increase in the nation's fluctuating gasoline prices? The fact is that if income is fixed and daily costs rise, where will the money come from to cover the higher price of gasoline and heating oil, electricity, or other utility costs?

Since 1993, the number of fully funded employer-sponsored health programs in the nation has dropped significantly, and these generous programs continue to decline. In fact, currently, only 18 percent of large employers contribute to the cost of covering health insurance for retirees younger than age sixty-five. This represents a marked decline from 30 percent as recently as 1993.

In addition, some U.S. companies have started to outsource production to subcontractors, which means these firms will no longer have to cover the cost of paying for health care to employees. In the short run, we are sure all prices in the nation will increase. The name for this is inflation.

Without added streams of income and with potential downturns in corporate dividend payments or lower-interest savings rates, how will tomorrow's seniors cover these cost increases when their incomes are diminished or depleted?

Past Expectations

Today's generation shares a pleasant memory of our fathers' and grandfathers' retirement one or two generations ago, a time when the options were limited and the cost of living comfortably was less. If you believe this memory represents your own retirement, you have not looked reality in the face.

In addition, the Pension Protection Act of 2006 changes all the rules. It doesn't protect much, but puts people on notice to save for their own retirement fund.

The need for extended years of income was significantly less for men of the past generations, who usually died in their early and mid sixties. In fact, a large percentage of these men never lived long enough to collect social security payments at age sixty-five.

Many of the current population over sixty probably met only one grandfather and enjoyed that grandpa's company for a short time. Frequently, our parents' households featured one grandmother who lived with the family. Granny came to live with us seemingly with enough money from savings, social security, and the sale of the family homestead to contribute to household expenses. Other siblings would often also contribute to her care. Even if she had to go to a nursing home, the cost for care long ago seemed reasonable.

Importantly, twenty-five years ago and earlier, there were fewer elderly people in the country. Those who needed nursing care could often find beds in state-run or charitable homes and others operated by religious groups. But today, as the number of seniors rises and the costs for assisted care have skyrocketed, this convenient and inexpensive method is no longer a solution for families faced with elderly parents with deteriorating health living on into their eighties or even nineties.

A generation later—in our parents' generation—many middle-class families could, upon Dad's retirement, sell the family home, possibly move south to the Sun Belt to buy a house or apartment in a warmer climate, and live free from the constant anxiety of income generation.

Those retirees who stayed in their original homes and did not head south lived in houses completely paid for and without mortgage debt. Whatever the total income from pensions, savings, and social security, the family that remained in its home had only local property taxes to pay. Without a burdensome monthly housing cost, most of these retirees retained sufficient income for expenses.

At Dad's death, often not so many years after his retirement, he left sufficient income for a surviving spouse, much of it in savings. Mom, who often lived for another five, ten, or fifteen years, had money to live, to pay for care in a nursing home, or to live with children without being a financial burden.

However, projections are not favorable that people fifty years and older today will have money to pay for the constantly rising costs of food, gasoline, medical care, drugs, and other expenses.

Apprehension

The closer people are to sixty-five, the more apprehensive they become when faced with the prospect of having no work and living off pensions, social security, and savings. Many have started taking social security at age sixty-two. This has also forced some seniors to take a hard look at their prospects for living either in semi- or full retirement.

Here—taken from our many interviews—are some serious concerns expressed by those approaching retirement.

Longevity Concerns

Living longer will be a blessing and a curse.

✔ "I will outlive my savings."
✔ "I have enough money to last until I'm eighty. After that it is the poorhouse for me."
✔ "My parents suffered chronic, late-in-life illnesses. If I, too, develop these diseases, how will I pay for medical care and drugs needed to keep me going?"
✔ "Will I have the funds to pay for an assisted living plan?"
✔ "Will I have monies for in-home nursing care?"
✔ "I have no children. Who will take care of me if I live to be eighty or ninety?

Penury Concerns

Monetary concerns will be a constant and anxiety-producing reminder of the daily costs of living in retirement.

✔ "I can barely make ends meet now when I'm working full time. What will happen when I stop work or am forced out of this job?"
✔ "My husband's illness ate up all of our savings."

✔ "My income is fixed, and each month some new drug cost goes up. I have to balance food and rent with keeping myself on these meds."

✔ "I shall become a financial burden to my children."

✔ "I'll have to keep working forever, and I'll die at my desk."

✔ "Will seniors, like unwanted newborn babies, be dropped off on the steps of churches and nursing homes, abandoned by their children?"

Past Expectation Concerns

Even many boomers have relied upon an outdated model for their retirement.

✔ "My pension plan evaporated when the company declared bankruptcy. I was counting on that money all my life for retirement."

✔ "The firm promised full medical benefits if I took early retirement, Now it reneged on these payments, and I have to pay $15,000 a year out-of-pocket."

✔ "Our company was bought out, and the new company said it would not honor past pension guarantees."

✔ "I always thought I would retire to Florida like my dad, play golf, and live in financial security. But now I see that I really can't afford even this minimal retirement."

✔ "I never thought that I would have to keep giving my children money for my grandchildren's college education."

Other Concerns

There are also many additional concerns that affect fifty-year-olds.

✔ "It is much harder to say to colleagues that you need to leave work early to change your father's incontinence pads than to say you are picking up your daughter from band practice."

✔ "I can't work because I'm needed at home to take care of my ninety-seven-year-old mother, who needs full-time attention."

✔ "I expected my husband's pension to continue in full after his death. I had never asked him what pension option he had chosen. Tragically, I later learned that he selected an option that gave us higher income while he was alive as opposed to continuing income for me as a widow."

The ReWorked Life

Insurance to Fly Fishing Coach

Rod McGarry had worked in the insurance industry ever since leaving college. While on this career path, he developed a sideline of motivational speaking and was often called upon to act as toastmaster for company events. Eventually he developed a reputation as someone who could motivate and teach other insurance personnel in lively and interactive presentations.

When it came time to retire, McGarry decided to move back to Portland, Maine, where his wife's family lived. But there was another, more central reason to his decision: As a fly fisherman all his life starting as a teenager in the Boy Scouts—and having used fly fishing as a metaphor for success in insurance sales—he had caught the attention of L.L. Bean, the famous catalog and outdoor clothing company located in Freeport, Maine, a short drive north from Portland.

The company recruited McGarry to be a summer instructor at the L.L. Bean Fly Fishing School. McGarry had found the ideal weekend position to indulge his love of the sport and to share his delight in teaching its techniques to others.

He is now a Registered Professional Maine Guide and one of only 140 people in the country who is a Board-Certified Master Fly-Casting Instructor. With this accreditation, he is licensed to take L.L. Bean's clients on overnight excursions or weeklong fly-fishing trips through the lakes and streams of Maine.

Rarely do retirees find the idyllic second career to do what they love to do at a leisurely pace—but Rod McGarry has.

Expert Advice: Psyching Up to Go Back to Work

You may regard returning to the workplace with some trepidation. Initially, a new workplace will be unknown, with unusual surroundings and unfamiliar people.

However, what is likely to cause the most anxiety will be the work itself, since it probably will be different from your previous occupation. You may fear that the skills acquired from your life-long career may have little or no application in a new job that will demand different performance standards. In short, your worry is that you will do subpar work. It may seem overly simplified, but in truth the key is to go to work exuding the same positive and proactive attitude that won you the job assignment.

Since so many seniors we talked to described the anxiety of starting anew—even though they were looking forward to the beginning of a new chapter in life—we thought it important to offer some practical tips to help navigate the emotional and psychological difficulties of the first day, or first week, back at work.

ReWorking Expert Advice

We asked Ann M. Patch, a psychologist and a senior, for her advice and counsel on what someone can expect in this situation, and how to handle the transition. In addition, we canvassed many of our contacts to dig out those real and imagined apprehensions that might inhibit a senior person from making a good start.

Here are Ann Patch's useful suggestions for "psyching up" before that return to the new job.

Be confident. You are a reliable worker and will make a constructive addition. Seniors are known for having excellent working skills. It doesn't matter if the work is new; years of past successes will help you do the job. You will also find that your reservoir of past skills and problem-solving techniques will help you in the new job situation. The expectations at your workplace are positive that you will succeed.

The ReWorked Life

Salesperson to Tour Guide

Karen Goodman says matter-of-factly that she's been "blown sideways through life." It is a three-act play in which the end of Act I left her a young widow with two small children, when, sadly, her husband died at age thirty-nine.

She had a background in art and photography but could not find sufficiently lucrative work. Instead, in the middle of Act II she became a salesperson for an office equipment company in New York City. She had great people skills and was good at organizing herself and associates.

She was assigned the training of new salespeople at the company's Manhattan office. With these out-of-towners in tow, she began impromptu architectural walking tours of the city.

In 1990, she attended the New York production of the play *Lettuce and Lovage*, with Dame Maggie Smith. The play dealt with a woman who decided to become a tour guide of historic houses. For Goodman, it was like seeing her life's ambition on stage. When the curtain came down, so did Act II in her professional life.

Act III began when she answered an advertisement for new tour guides. She qualified, was trained by the company, and passed her license requirements with the New York City Department of Consumer Affairs.

Since then, she has led student and adult tours from Georgia to Maine by motor coach. Over time, her reputation, friendliness, and organizing skills have been recognized by local and out-of-town tour companies, which book her regularly.

Because the tour guide business is seasonal, she has also developed an ancillary business as a professional closet organizer, a possible Act IV in a productive life.

Ask questions. Know that other people will be helpful in areas that you do not understand. Recall when mentors lent you a hand at the beginning of an earlier job. These helpful people exist at the new job also. The company or organization knows that often the job presents new tasks with which you are unfamiliar. Either you will have a short training schedule or, more probably, someone experienced will be assigned to assist you through the first weeks, frequently working alongside you until you have mastered the basics.

Take your time. Remember that it will seem strange at first. You will need a period of adjustment to become acclimated to everything. We all suffer minor uneasiness with the new until, over time, we have absorbed it into our consciousness. The fear, normal and real, will evaporate over time. The more positive you are that this workplace will become a place of reward and satisfaction, the greater the probability that the nervousness will fade away.

Avoid stress. This is particularly important if the job seems similar to your past employment. You do not want to carry over into the new job the old bugaboos that caused stress in the past. These represented conditions that may have motivated you to do good work (e.g., striving to get ahead, competition with coworkers, power, status, etc.), but you can do a great job without resurrecting motivational anxiety.

List your goals. To be more productive at the job, make a list of a few short-term and weekly attainable objectives. This will enable you to concentrate on what's important. In addition, the goal-orientation will generate satisfaction as each objective is achieved. You will find work richer and more enjoyable.

Be outgoing. Try to meet other people your own age. Meeting and befriending others your age at the workplace will establish a new network of people with feelings and experience similar to your own.

Don't overcriticize. One of the most annoying and recurrent of mistakes at the new job is to refer constantly to how well things were done at your past career job. The past was yesterday. Concentrate on making some minor suggestions on little matters. You'll find that your advice will be sought on the big things.

Assess yourself. After a month, it is important to review the satisfaction levels with the new job. Foremost, how does it make you feel—not only on the job, but when you are home. If it fills you with negative emotions (e.g., boredom, discomfort) or it has become too physically trying, then consider how you can restructure the job to reduce these harmful outcomes.

If it seems like drudgery, quit. Why keep doing something that you detest? If it provides no satisfaction and is, in fact, taking a toll on you mentally and physically, then leave at the first opportunity. There's always another job out there somewhere that can provide similar pay and less negativity.

* * *
A Final Note

Facts should be your only guide to the new reality of retirement. Examine likely retirement scenarios, and take another look at work as a possibility. Remember, if the answer to the age-old question "Do you need the money?" is yes, you will need to find new work to pay for expenses. But even among those who are well off or think that they are well off in retirement, work is something many want to continue.

2 Financial Planning

*"I've got all the money I'll ever need if
I die by four o'clock this afternoon."*

—Henny Youngman

It is important to do some earnest thinking and detailed planning regarding your retirement finances. The goal is to outlive your money. The more financial facts you gather and examine today, the more informed you will be for the many years on your retirement road ahead. Today's data will determine whether work should continue for you in the same job or whether you should seek other part-time or full-time work. Or you may enjoy the option of ceasing to work forever.

The oft-mentioned observation of Benjamin Franklin that "in this world nothing can be said to be is certain except death and taxes" could include the postscript "and it is a 100 percent certainty that all living costs will increase as time passes." Every chart comparing the prices of gasoline, college education, home buying, etc. shows a continued and often steep rise over time.

Has earning capacity kept pace with the escalating costs of living? This is the crux of the problem for people turning fifty and older: How much income will be needed for the next twenty to thirty years ahead, and where will it be found?

That leads to another crucial question: Will income from the formerly rock-solid "three-legged stool" of retirement income— social security, savings, and pensions—be enough to meet the expenses of tomorrow?

And what if at some future point, social security can only fund 75 percent or down to 50 percent of its obligation? What will you do if there's a shortfall in the fund when your time arrives to start collecting? If this occurs, then replacement money will be needed to maintain a modest lifestyle especially for those retirees mainly dependant only on social security income.

Sources of Retirement Income

It will be helpful to cite briefly the sources available when you consider retirement to accurately figure out your potential to earn future income.

- ✔ **Savings**—Money in savings accounts, money markets, IRA accounts, and any other accumulation of cash.
- ✔ **Pensions**—Employer-defined benefit plans. In some cases, you may be eligible for more than one pension from multiple employers. It is important to check the amount coming to you while you are still employed. Note that there is no guarantee that pension funds will be available for you when you are ready to retire.
- ✔ **Social security payments**—We reiterate: It is vital for you to understand all the options presented by this agency, particularly how to access payments as early as age sixty-two. Non-working married women should understand death benefits, when these begin, and at what percentage.
- ✔ **Employer-defined plans**—These are the 401(k) and 403(b) plans, in which the employee invested pretax funds that were matched or invested by the company. You cannot access this money until age fifty-nine.
- ✔ **Work**—Are you still employed? What are the wages coming to you over the next few years? Is there a mandatory retirement age? If yes, money will cease at that moment.

Making a telephone call or going online is the easiest way to start the process of applying to social security with all of its many options and combinations of benefits.

The main telephone number to call is 1-800-772-1213. Based on our experience, we suggest that you also locate the social security office nearest your home. Call the 800 number listed above, or to find your local office online, go to the lower left-hand column of the main Social Security Administration page and type in your Zip Code. Keep the address and telephone number of this local office handy.

The SSA Web site at *www.socialsecurity.gov* (or *www.ssa.gov*) is packed with instructions and information. At first, it seems daunting to navigate the many areas and search segments, but if you can limit the parameters of your search, it can easily direct you to the information needed. Importantly, the agency has done its homework, anticipating the different questions a claimant will have, and all these queries can be answered online.

The application process is extraordinarily simple and streamlined. Once the process kicks in, it is easy to receive money on time, particularly if you request direct bank deposit.

Your social security payouts will factor into your income stream and serve as a base sum to determine how much more income you'll need to cover expenses. It is important to have the agency verify and authenticate information, since changes in age, payments, and collection change every year.

ReWorking Expert Advice

Social Security

We asked Social Security personnel to provide answers to some basic questions about starting social security, and to other related questions that might be asked about the program.

Q. *I receive a statement from Social Security around my birthday. What is it all about?*

A. Annually, everyone who pays into social security receives a form letter listing total earnings to date for all the years the individual has been paying into the fund. The key suggestion is to check this statement each year to make sure the information is correct.

Q. *How can I calculate what I'll receive in the future?*

A. Online at *www.ssa.gov*, you can use the benefit calculator to figure out what monies you will receive and when. If you telephone, the information will be given over the phone, and you can request also that it be mailed to you.

Q. *What identification do I need to start the process of applying for social security?*

A. Acceptable forms of identification are birth certificate or other proofs of birth, citizen naturalization papers, U.S. military discharge papers, W-2 forms and/or self-employment tax forms from the previous year.

For the birth certificate and certain other documents, the agency insists on original documentation and will never accept a photocopy. If you lost or misplaced the original birth certificate, you will have to obtain it from the state or country in which you were born. You must check with that state to inquire about the handling process.

A helpful hint from Social Security: do not delay filing even if you do not have the documentation; the agency can and will assist you in obtaining them. All documents will be returned to you.

Q. *I'm confused. I can't start taking full social security at sixty-five, as in the past. Does this mean I can't start receiving early benefits at age sixty-two?*

A. No, even though the age of generating the full rate advances every year and, most probably, the age will continue to move forward in future years. Look at this chart to find when you can start:

Year of Birth When You Can Start Social Security

Year of birth	Age
1937 or before	65
1938	65 and two months
1939	65 and four month
1940	65 and six months
1941	65 and eight month
1942	65 and ten months
1943–1954	66
1955	66 and two months
1956	66 and four months
1957	66 and six months
1958	66 and eight months
1960 and after	67

Remember, this is for full benefits. Social Security still allows seniors to begin receiving partial benefits at age sixty-two.

Q. *Should I plan to visit my local Social Security office to start the procedure?*

A. The answer is no. To start the process, a telephone call or going online represent quick and efficient methods that can be followed up by regular mail.

Local offices handle many procedures other than the start-up process, and you could arrive on a crowded day when the line is long. But if you perceive that making personal contact will answer all of your individual questions, call for an appointment first. Do not just stop in.

Q. *What are the maximum ranges of monthly payments?*

A. In 2006, the maximum amount was $2,052 per individual. At this amount, non-working spouses, (if they were the same age) could qualify for social security and receive $1,026 in their own name. This couple's monthly combined income then would come to $3,078 a month, or a total of $36,936 for the year.

If a spouse also worked and both were of an age to receive full benefits—and both qualified for the maximum allowable benefit—this working couple would receive $4,104 in joint income or $49, 248 annually.

Keep these social security maximum sums in mind: One working person equals $2,052 per month, or $24,624 annually. A working and non-working spouse equals $36, 936. And the case where both spouses worked and qualified for the maximum, it would come to $49,248.

These monthly sums will increase after the annual reassessment of the cost of living index, which can be checked at the agency's Web site in the fall months to find out how much additional money will be coming the next year.

Q. *I plan to retire to another country. How do I collect my social security?*

A. Briefly, the same way you do here—payments by check or by direct bank deposit. But the agency has different rules for payments to different countries and our strong advice is to contact Social Security to learn the specific regulations about each country. Online, in the Search box on top, scroll down to International Issues.

Q. *Is my social security payment taxable?*

A. The answer is yes, in some instances, depending on what you earn from other sources during the year. At the end of the year, you will receive SSA-1099 from the agency, which will indicate how much social security income was paid. This is no different from other 1099 income statements.

If you want to learn more about how much other income you can earn, go to the Internal Revenue Service Web site at *www.IRS .gov*. Then go to Frequently Asked Questions, which will take you to a list, and find Social Security Income. There are explanations and worksheets in IRS jargon. Request Form 915, which explains in greater detail when you will have a tax liability on social security income. Many retirees are surprised when they learn that in many instances, they have to pay tax on social security income.

Q. *I speak another language more fluently than English. Can I find out about social security in my native tongue?*

A. Yes, Social Security maintains a staff that is bilingual in local ethnic areas. It prints versions of all its booklets and Web offerings in Spanish, the second-largest language group in America, and it prints some of the more commonly used booklets in other languages as well.

However, if an applicant speaks a foreign language that cannot be handled by a local translator, Social Security can arrange telephone assistance in that person's language. These calls are done by appointment, and usually with the assistance of a friend or family member who speaks English or Spanish.

Q. *What happens if I disagree with the amount of money Social Security intends to pay me?*

A. The agency has a fair appeals process that allows you to contest their decision.

Retirement Planning 101

Perhaps early retirement was precipitated by a company layoff, and as a result it came years before you were ready for it. Or maybe you had anticipated retirement for a long time and were able to retire on your own terms. In either case, it is important to look at the financial and psychological aspects of what the future holds.

One of the obligatory steps is to do a budget-planning assignment that looks at projected income and projected expenses. For a more detailed, in-depth guide we recommend the excellent book *Retirement Planning* by Lita Epstein, which has more than 350 pages of helpful tips and hints with lots of useful exercises. Also, there are many software packages to assist you in the retirement exercises. These come from Fidelity, Quicken, Vanguard, and others as well.

You have to complete a retirement calculator exercise if you are serious about planning for the future. It may seem like a tedious chore, but even educated guesses are more productive than not filling in the worksheet. Tip: Do it in sections, a little bit every day, so it does not seem so burdensome.

A hard look at your financial reality can determine whether it is time to make the important decisions about retirement. Looking at the bottom line, is it necessary for you to continue work because of a deficit between anticipated income and expenses? If you need to work, will it be full time or part time to fill in the income differential?

If an income gap does exist, how wide is it? Is it small and manageable, and can breakeven be met with a reduction in some minor expenses? What fat can you trim from the budget? What annual expenses are unimportant enough to do without? Are you willing to make small sacrifices in order not to work—e.g., cut out a second vacation, delay the purchase of a new car, reduce charitable contributions, stop sending generous cash gifts to children?

Note that reduction in your expenses can be a smart strategy to help level your income through retirement. The problem for you may come further down the road if some calamity occurs and you are too infirm to look for new work.

Choices

If you have planned well for the financial future, you'll have an income surplus and will not need to work for income. At this point in your life it is time to make other decisions:

✔ Do you want to move to a retirement community?
✔ Does your spouse join you in this retirement and moving decision?
✔ Where are children and grandchildren living, and how far away from your preferred place of retirement?
✔ What will you do during your retirement, and will you need another activity to fill your time or aid your psychological/ emotional well-being?

It is also time for you to look at your financial picture and consider lifetime giving or leaving an inheritance to heirs or to charitable institutions. The question is when and how much? If now, these funds will not be available to you for income generation. Most retirees, for reasons of income security, hold off the final giving until death.

Financial Reasons for Working in Retirement

There are basic scenarios in which you might need or want to work in retirement:

1. The budget and income work sheets you filled out reveal a major monetary discrepancy. If the difference is a bottom-line deficit on what is minimally needed to live, there is no choice but to find work to make up the shortage. While searching for new work, it is prudent to settle for any job that generates some income.
2. You have planned well, and no gap exists. In fact, you have a surplus, which leaves extra income for discretionary purchases. Now reasons for considering working are different: You need a little spending money for extra travel. You need work to fill in long hours of no activity.
3. You have been financially successful and can be considered well off or even wealthy, with no current or potential future income problem. You still want to fill your days with something more than golf or television. Do you have enough money to fulfill a dream? Buy a franchise operation for the family? Do volunteer work?

A word of caution about doing retirement spreadsheets: The greatest potential future strain on income can come from unplanned escalating or catastrophic health-care costs. Medical or nursing home expenses can damage any planning projection. If family history or your own medical past reveals the probability of a serious illness, then the work you find today will provide more monies. Devastating illness can strike anyone at any time.

Investment Strategies for Retirement

The answer to the question of how much money you need is that there is no set answer. Each case is different, and one family situation is not comparable to another. No one can predict the future, particularly investment returns. The stock market could fall, real estate could tumble, or a nationwide recession could occur, bringing with it economic doomsday scenarios.

We say, beware of investment articles that indicate different income need multipliers for the future because the people who estimate these numbers want to switch your money to their products. These articles will assert that X years from retirement, the cost to maintain a lifestyle should be multiplied by Y. These are merely estimates, and there is no assurance these multipliers are accurate, whether they're predicting five or twenty-five years into the future.

Here are some basic options for what to do with your income:

Option One: Be strictly conservative in outlook.

The overriding goal is to preserve principal. Convert all assets to investments with little or no inflation protection. Examples are government bonds, savings accounts, and CDs. This strategy can be successful if you possess a sufficiently large number of assets to protect against inflation. Note that all your expenses are going to inflate. Even if your mortgage is paid off, property taxes will increase.

Option Two: Place assets in high-quality mutual funds.

You want funds that have a long history of buying stock and bonds in a periodic plan. Most financial planners feel comfortable with around a 4 percent rate of withdrawal. This kind of planning offers inflation protection and an inheritance. The IRS requires mandatory distributions from qualified retirement plans (IRAs or 401(k)s) after age seventy and six months.

Option Three: Develop a growth strategy.

This option is for those who envision retirement as a long-term goal and want to stay well ahead of inflation and increase their asset base for any contingency. The objective is to maintain or improve lifestyle and to leave a larger inheritance. The portfolio will be skewed to equity investments in both large and small cap stocks and real estate. The more conservative the investment, the larger the inflation risk you accept. The more growth-oriented, the larger investment risk there is.

Obtaining Financial Advice

It is beyond the scope of this book to turn you into a professional retirement planner. After having budgeted and examined finances for the future, it is important for you to have a financial/investment roadmap. Questions about insurance, taxes, investments, and medical costs are important aspects of this planning.

It may be possible for some to do this alone through reading the many books available, attending financial planning seminars, watching business and investment television programs, and finding advice on the Internet. It is still a good idea to ask for expert financial advice.

Retirement financial planning is difficult and often confusing. Our advice is to research different financial companies, looking for someone who has a history of advising retirees. Make sure that all of those you contact offer a full range of financial products.

✔ **Banks**—If you have developed a good, long-term banking relationship with a banking institution you trust, this should be the first place to seek advice. Often banks will try to sell CDs and annuities or their own family of mutual funds.

✔ **Stock brokerage firms**—If you have had profitable experience in the stock market, you should explore what investment firms have to offer. Often these institutions will sponsor financial seminars advertised via a direct mail piece or the newspapers. Most likely, brokers will try to place most of your money into individual stocks and bonds.

✔ **Financial planners**—This is a broad category and includes insurance agents, certified public accountants, tax specialists, lawyers, and licensed individuals from the accredited College for Financial Planning. A cautionary note: Anyone can use the title "financial planner."

Other Sources of Financial Advice

In seeking financial advice, be cautious and sensible. If you're invited to attend a financial seminar, for instance, find out what the sponsors are selling. Remember the adages "There is no such thing as a free lunch" and "Buyer beware." Also remember "If it sounds too good to be true, it is."

The ReWorked Life

CFO to Major League President

Michael Herman worked as the Chief Financial Officer at Marion Labs, the pharmaceutical company founded by Ewing Kauffman. When Merrill Dow acquired Marion Labs in 1989, it allowed Herman to cash in stock options and to devote his newly found retirement to volunteer and philanthropic work.

His first task was to redirect funds to Kansas City's inner-city schools, formulating programs to keep children drug-free and on a college-bound course.

Kauffman was also the owner of the Kansas City Royals, winners of the World Series in 1980 and 1985. In 1989, with the team's success declining, Kauffman turned the presidency over to Herman with instructions to keep the club (now losing money) in Kansas City.

Herman had to keep the Royals in town and pare costs. Major League Baseball rejected his first idea of giving the team to Kansas City as a gift. Then he conceived an original concept: he created a charity that became the owner of the Royals. But there was a catch. Since the team was now owned by a charity, no salaries could be given to the officers of the team. Herman had to pay for his own seats and hot dogs at Royals' games to demonstrate that he accepted no perks from the charity.

By 2001, the team's finances had improved, and Herman auctioned off the club to David Glass, a former Wal-Mart executive who had served as the Royals' CEO. The sale netted $166 million to the charity, which continued doing good work.

Questions to Ask Professionals:

The following questions will help you select a qualified professional financial planner. The key is to have a high degree of trust and confidence in her.

- ✔ What are her background and qualifications in retirement planning?
- ✔ What is the history of the company?
- ✔ What specifically does the advisor or her company offer as the main product?
- ✔ What is her primary philosophy of retirement finances (e.g., overly conservative versus excessively aggressive)?
- ✔ Who will work on the account today and, importantly, who will be working on it in the future?
- ✔ How is the advisor or firm remunerated?
- ✔ How are charges determined (e.g., commissions, fees, annual percentage of assets, hourly rate, or a blend of some or all of the above)?
- ✔ Has the advisor or the firm ever been disciplined by the regulatory authorities (e.g., National Association of Securities Dealers, Securities and Exchange Commission, Certified Financial Planner Board, or others)? A would-be investor can check disciplinary history online at *www.cfp.net* or *www.finra.org*.
- ✔ What exists in writing about the nature of the customer's future relationship with the firm or advisor?

✔ Does the firm or advisor have any conflicts of interest with any recommendations (e.g., an insurance agent who only offers his company's products)?

It is important for couples to be involved jointly in this planning from the beginning. Husband and wife must share confidence in the same planner and the goals set out for retirement. In all probability, one person will outlive the other, and the surviving spouse needs to be comfortable with the financial planning advisor, the firm, and most importantly, the concept for investment.

A time will come when you will decide to consider seriously the financial ramifications of retirement. At that point, you will take the necessary steps to review your income and expense picture. You may consult investment counselors and retirement specialists, purchase special books, or download online spreadsheet plans from insurance or other finance-related companies. You may talk to people with expertise.

Many of us procrastinate, putting off the decision for another day. Examining the future can be a depressing exercise and speaks to our mortality. Another reason is the realization that there may not be adequate money to retire, which sets off a wave of stress and anxiety and self-recrimination about spending and savings mistakes made in the past.

Financial planning for retirement, with its many contingencies, has to be completed before people reach fifty. Those sixty and sixty-five years old should continue to evaluate their financial future. (Some advise starting as early as forty, but we find this to be overly conservative.) Avoidance and procrastination are the twin negatives that hold many people back from completing this necessary assignment.

ReWorking Expert Advice

Financial Planning

We invited financial expert Joe Frank to provide specific investment tools for financial planning. He will take you through the real world of how to become financially independent for the uncertain future. And he believes in the old proverb "If you do not have a plan, you are just gambling."

Understand the Psychology of Retirement

The foremost reason why retirement is so stressful is that a decision made late in life is forever. Rarely are there any do-overs. Not enough time remains to make up for poor financial choices. Sell the house, and it is gone as an asset. Pick a stock in a company that goes down, and there will not be years ahead to find replacement income.

In addition, the fear of making a mistake often prevents you from making any decisions. The two outcomes from the process lead to negative results: either you spend too much money or, conversely, you spend too little. The one good solution is smart financial planning for the future.

Manage Risks

The protection of assets remains the most important concern. All assets have varying degrees of risk, and it is never possible to eliminate risk totally. One way to pare down or reduce the risk is by having a blend of assets in the investment portfolio.

Essentially there are six major kinds of risk:

1. Inflation, or the loss of future purchasing power
2. Business risk, or the decrease in value of a company that underperforms
3. Market risk, or a decline in the worth of certain equities
4. Interest rates risk, or a drop in the prime rate and other lending variables that determine what businesses have to pay to borrow money

5. Payment of unnecessary taxes, or poorly considered calculations that do not understand the different tax consequences of single and blended investments

6. Liquidity, or the degree to which an asset or security can be bought or sold in the market without affecting its price or the capacity to convert an asset to cash

Build a Balanced Portfolio

The strategy to combat the negative elements of risk is to build a balanced portfolio that can add value to the assets and reduce the threat of keeping only one asset and experience a significant loss if it declines. The savvy person will diversify among several asset classes, including fixed annuities, bonds, and publicly traded real estate investment trusts (REITs). Other short-term investments not subject to risk are certificates of deposit (CDs), Treasury or T-bills, and money market funds. These latter investments should be considered parking places for money until other, longer-term strategies are chosen.

Hold Annuities

The advantage of buying annuities is that taxation is deferred on income until it is finally received. A good rule of thumb is that taxation tomorrow is better than being taxed today. Basically, there are three types of annuities: single-premium immediate annuities (SPIAs), standard fixed annuities, and fixed indexed annuity. In all three, an investor cannot lose the principal or the earned interest. One caution: Annuities can be subject to surrender penalties if cashed in before the contract matures.

Hold Bonds

Bonds are useful investment tools for two primary reasons: they generate income, and they are predictable. If you hold a ten-year bond, the cash flow every year can be easily calculated and the amount of annual income known. After maturity, you will receive the face value of the bond, and it will be returned to you.

However, certain bonds present two potential pitfalls: the credit-worthiness of the issuer and the fluctuation of long-term bonds from periodic changes in the interest rates.

Managing Taxes During Retirement

The key to reducing your tax liability is to comprehend the consequences of various types of a blended portfolios, since the IRS treats these differently. One rule to keep in mind is to try to avoid paying taxes on any monies not in current use. Possible complications also arise when retirees start to collect social security income, which is occasionally subject to taxation.

The ReWorked Life

Sales Exec to Manufacturer

Jon Prusmack started his career as an artist. He liked the freelancing life but realized that while he was working on one project, he had to be pitching the next one. He searched for something tangible to sell.

In his mid-forties, he began exporting prepackaged medical supplies to the Middle East. A Saudi Arabian client asked if Prusmack could also supply easy-to-mount field hospitals. Prusmack could not find a shelter system that was lightweight and easy to move while accommodating the needs of the hospital.

He believed he would have a product to manufacture and sell if he could solve the design problems. With his wife, he created a new shelter system modeled after existing geodesic designs used in exhibits at trade shows.

Prusmack, at fifty, was financially leveraged to the maximum. There were no sales for the start-up company. He was faced with the sad possibility of a dream denied and returning to a life of freelance creative projects.

But he had built a better, more efficient shelter system, and soon the military started to buy in small quantities. He developed more diverse models of his portable shelters, and more sales ensued, some from overseas.

Today the company, called DHS Logistics, employs 300 people and has factories in New York, Alabama, and Hereford, UK. Prusmack has also added climatization and computer command and control to the shelters, offering the Department of Defense a complete shelter-system package.

Prusmack thought that if he ever found a single product that sold well, he would retire in his sixties. But the joy of growing the company and creating new products keeps the sixty-five-year-old motivated every day. (In late 2007, look for a sleek recreational and tailgating camper sold under the name "C.A.M.P. Inc.")

Have Specific Time Frames for Investments

You should divide the next twenty years into four five-year sections. This exercise follows the first financial analysis of retirement when you calculated the money to be received from social security, pensions, and other sources. The following time chart will indicate the parameters for these four different time blocks:

1. **Years one to five**—Cash, money market, EE bonds, CDs, T-bills, short-term bonds, savings, SPIAs
2. **Years six to ten**—Intermediate-term bonds, fixed and indexed annuities, REITs, SPIAs, income funds
3. **Years eleven to fifteen**—Long-term bonds, income/growth and balanced mutual funds, variable annuities, REITs, SPIAs
4. **Years sixteen to twenty**—Growth-oriented mutual funds, individual stocks such as XOM or IBM

How the Time Periods Work to Your Advantage

Let's examine these four time periods to see why each one contains different investments.

1. **First Level (years one to five)**—These investments are made up primarily of cash and instruments that can be converted into cash within five years. This guarantees income needs regardless of fluctuations, because in the short term the yield will keep pace with the pace of inflation.
2. **Second Level (years six to ten)**—Since these instruments will not kick in until the sixth year, their yield will exceed inflation by one to three percentage points.
3. **Third Level (years eleven to fifteen)**—These instruments do not have to be liquidated until the eleventh year. The estimate is that they will produce interest levels from 6.5 percent to 8.5 percent, amounts higher than the anticipated increase of inflation.
4. **Fourth Level (years sixteen to twenty)**—Historically, these investments have significantly outpaced inflation by 5 or 6 percentage points. Additionally, these kinds of instruments are often cyclically driven, and it takes ten to twelve years to pass through cycles. Finally, in the long term these investments will probably beat inflation.

Actual Returns on Investment Options

Financial data on investment return has been gathered for more than eighty years. The key lesson over this time is that it is a mistake to liquidate equity investments when they decline. Short-term market conditions traditionally will have a negative impact on the equities market, causing periodic decreases in worth. But you, as the savvy investor, are always geared for the long term, and that it why it is not advisable to sell equities because they decrease in value in the short term.

Here is how returns on investments have fared over the past eighty years. The numbers are taken from Ibbotson Associates Stocks, Bonds, Bills, and Inflation (SBBI) 2005 Yearbook. The rate of inflation for this same period averaged 3.1 percent.

Returns on Investment

Small Company Stocks	17.5 percent
Prestige Company Stocks	12.4 percent
Long-Term Corporate Bonds	6.2 percent
Long-Term Government Bonds	5.8 percent
Intermediate Term Government Bonds	5.5 percent
U.S. Treasury Bills	3.8 percent

It is dangerous to go into an uncertain financial future without professional advice. Consult with an investment-planning professional and talk to your banker. Explore all contingencies.

A Final Note

Checking finances is the key to determining whether you need to work during retirement. No matter how well you save or invest money in a variety of plans, no one knows the variables of tomorrow. Work remains the one certain way to keep ahead of possible declines in investments and continually rising costs.

3 ReWorking Work

*"I'm living so far beyond my income that
we may almost be said to be living apart."*

—E.E. Cummings

Working is the best way for you to narrow the gap between expenses and income. Working is not just a question of getting a paycheck; it is also a question of how much money you need and for how long.

Aside from the financial benefit, work can also promote good mental and physical health. All studies indicate that people over fifty years old who work have healthier bodies. And older people who work suffer fewer other physical problems such as depression, heart disease, and hypertension.

Work in later years stimulates your mind and is a wonderful social activity that keeps you connected. If you find some activity that you like—perhaps postponed while you experienced another career—it can make every day one of enjoyment. For those people with financial security, work becomes an opening to explore new commercial, artistic, or altruistic opportunities.

Potential Problems Seeking Work

The opportunities for finding new employment are hindered by the fact that you are an older person. That may be a harsh reality, but it's true. Every day someone says, "Oh, sixty is the new forty" or, "Fifty is the new thirty." Exercise and healthier diets have brought about healthier lifestyles and longer lives. But the truth is and has always been that fifty means fifty, particularly, when compared to people who actually are thirty. And studies show that corporate America mainly wants to invest dollars and resources to train younger people because they will be around many more years than workers fifty years and older.

Some impediments you may encounter in seeking new employment are:

Bias against hiring. Younger colleagues may not want to have what they perceive as surrogate parents or people from yesterday's generation around the work environment

Inflexibility of the employer. You want flexible work schedules to fit into retirement plans along with a desire for limited hours of work per week. You also have different health concerns, extended vacation plans, and other age-related matters that future employers may not want to grant.

Cutbacks in the work force. Many segments of American industry have downsized or outsourced work to other countries. Consequently, many of these companies have forced their employees to take early retirement, often without extension of medical benefits or options to stay on group medical plans. The net result is that jobs have diminished in many of these sectors. If cutbacks do occur, it is often older workers who are the first to go.

Competition with younger workers. Companies looking to grow will invariably hire younger employees who possess the energy and interest to become employees for the long term.

Seniors' resistance. This is a catchall for the many areas of new work that may generate negative and uncooperative responses from older workers. It includes reluctance to do low-paying jobs, learn new technology, work at all hours, and take orders from those younger than themselves.

The ReWorked Life

Teaching Full-Time to Flexible Teaching

Harvey Stick returned to teach science at the same high school in New Jersey from which he graduated. He credited the school with giving him a love of learning, and he wanted to instill this same passion for science in the students.

After teaching for more than twenty years Stick analyzed his pension and decided it was worth his while to take early retirement. He looked forward to a pleasant life of tennis and skiing.

Over time, the nation had experienced a significant shortfall of new high school science teachers. Many of those entering the system annually tended to be liberal arts teachers. As older science teachers retired, towns and cities all across America were desperate to find qualified science teachers to fill the demand.

Stick received a request from his old high school to become a substitute teacher for a few days. Then the school asked him to commit for twelve weeks to replace a teacher on maternity leave. Stick quoted the school district a fair price, but it declined his proposal and, instead, offered a lower amount. He did not need the money, and he walked away from the offer.

The school could not find a substitute for the class and offered a higher salary amount closer to Stick's original quote. He went back to teaching the course.

Stick is an example of senior skills that become scarce and continue to be in demand. He had to decide at what price he was willing to trade free time for work time.

Work Overview—Considering Retirement

If you are fifty years old or older, you will likely have had serious thoughts about finishing your career. This important work-ending decision—whenever it comes—will compel you to look at the concept of retirement, perhaps for the first time. It is ironic that people will spend more time planning a daughter's wedding or a vacation than planning for the last quarter of their lives.

Some important questions to ask are:

✔ Have you made detailed retirement plans?
✔ Did you factor in working full time, part time, or not working at all?
✔ Have recent changes in anticipated retirement benefits, projected medical charges, a rising cost of living (including rising housing prices), and other economic, personal, or medical variables altered your carefully considered plans?

Or have you already stopped working and now the day-to-day inactivity of doing nothing has become the proverbial albatross of boredom around your neck? Is every day of retirement starting to look like the last one? Will tomorrow be a repeat of today, similar to the déjà vu in the movie *Groundhog Day?* It is time to look again at work options not only for income generation but also, importantly, for fulfillment.

ReWorking Expert Advice

The overwhelming goal of Americans who turn fifty is to stay working. Often, the best way to achieve this objective is to remain in the same career or industry.

We asked Angelo Sinisi, VP and General Manager of Laars Corporation, a well-known heating company, for his tips on why older workers should stay within the same career or remain with the same company. Sinisi had semi-retired and was doing some consulting when he was offered the chance to become the general manager. Today, he's back to working a fifty-hour week and is more energized than ever.

Anxiety about income, medical benefits, and quality of life will induce or compel many older workers to remain in the same career for as long as possible. This will prove a mixed bag of benefits, doing the same old job but without the matching enthusiasm of earlier years. Although boomers have tended to be more workcentric than older generations, holding onto a faded or unappetizing career merely to bring home a paycheck carries with it potential stress and disappointment.

Studies indicate that older employees will be more likely to remain on the job if they are in charge of their hours, find adaptable conditions at the workplace, and are given some work autonomy.

Sinisi believes you should first examine the pluses and minuses of the ongoing career before switching to a new one. The following lists his recommendations as to why staying with the career makes good sense.

It continues income generation. A basic fact is that industry will pay more for experience. A seasoned worker has established success, and those years of experience will continue to generate high paychecks. In addition, the current job will probably pay more than a new one in another industry, especially if you are starting out.

It maintains health benefits. You should stay on the company medical plan as long as possible, even if you have to pick up part of the cost. The company's medical coverage will be the best value for the money and less expensive than choosing private, individual plans. Remember, Medicare does not begin for you until age sixty-five.

You receive increased pension payments. Each year at the company increases equity in the IRA or 401(k) plan. Once you retire or change jobs, the money ceases to be reinvested in the plan. The longer you can postpone quitting the job, the larger will be your pension share when the day comes that you do exit the company.

You're good at this job. It makes sense to continue to do what you have enjoyed all your life. Maybe the familiarity has bred contempt. And the dream you may have nurtured all your life to do something else may require years of learning or costly retraining, or may be in a field that is already crowded with other experienced workers.

It extends lifelong social contacts. For many careerists who work at the same company, it has become a place where "everybody knows your name." You will prolong the familiar routine of lifelong coworker friends.

A new job or new venture will create stress. The new is often strange and worrisome and you will have to prove yourself again. In the current job, you are familiar with the markers for success. Why trade these in for new worries about job performance?

The career is something you enjoy. By this stage of life, you are doing—or should be doing—what you take pleasure in. You know the good things and the bad things about the job.

It keeps the power and the prestige. At the current job, you have reached a prominent status and enjoy the respect of others. In addition, you are part of the leadership team making decisions at the very highest level.

And you have built up a network of industry associates who know your value and worth. Trade this in for something new and you become a forgotten nobody.

The company or organization needs you. Your career is a valuable asset. It will prove costly and time-consuming for the company to replace you with all your years of experience. You possess knowledge that no one else has, and this expertise and know-how have great worth to the organization.

Career work will delay plans to consider retirement. The advantage of staying on the job and committing to it is that it will defer for a long time the decision to retire or think about retirement.

The ReWorked Life

Music Executive to Dental Receptionist

As a teenager growing up in North Carolina, Jess Marlow always looked forward to the weekend when her parents' copy of the thick Sunday *New York Times* arrived. And it was to New York City that she headed after graduating college.

Her first job was in the advertising department of RCA. She did not know then that she would remain with this company for the next twenty-five years. She eventually landed in the music catalog department, handling the recordings of the famed NBC Symphony Orchestra. She was asked to take over the entire Elvis Presley catalog, a job that entailed talking frequently to the legendary Colonel Tom Parker.

Marlow was promoted to the head of the sales promotion department and worked this job until General Electric Company acquired RCA. She opted for early retirement when GE offered a lucrative buy-out package.

She was determined to stay in New York City, whose cultural expectations exceeded her youthful fantasies. She tried real estate brokering for five years, but it was more hectic and stressful than she had anticipated.

She wanted an interesting job involving people, but where was it? Finally she became a receptionist for an Upper East Side Manhattan dentist whose clientele included artists and writers.

Marlow maintains the dental office in as efficient detail as an extensive musical catalog. What pleases many of the dentist's patients is discussing theater, opera, film, and museums with th sophisticated receptionist.

Are Eminently Employable

nation's economists believe that people older than age fifty present a significantly large and growing labor resource in the country. Employers will have no choice but to dip into this expanding and experienced labor pool for qualified workers in all areas of business.

In years past, age sixty-five marked the end of careers when workers were forced to retire. Ironically, the past elimination of seniors from the work force came about because of the large boomer population waiting in the wings to move up the ladder and assume managerial and seniority jobs

The nation's work force is graying primarily because older workers possess proved skills that the marketplace needs, whether full time or part time. There are five reasons to feel good about your future working potential.

Experience—You are well-trained with excellent lifetime skills. The aging pool of talent is sizable and increasing. In addition, in many technical areas in science and engineering, there is a scarcity of trained personnel, and only seniors with experience can fill this scientific shortfall.

Better health—The current generation of seniors is in good physical condition thanks to fitness regimens, nutrition, and advances in medicine. Employers are confident that you have the stamina and mental capacity to do the job.

Flexibility—Employers realize that you have neither the desire nor the energy to work full-time. Smarter companies have fashioned flexible schedules to accommodate the needs of these older workers.

Technology—So much of modern work is computer-based that people with technical skills are able to work at home on projects and electronically hand in assignments.

Not in the head count—Older workers working part time (less than twenty hours) or full time through "consulting" institutions do not figure in the company's employee head count. This allows the employer to look lean to Wall Street. The company benefits from excellent work and keeps the investment bankers happy with a low employee-to-revenue ratio.

Again, the real world recognizes the benefits that you offer such as experience, stability, enhanced knowledge, flexibility, credibility, and strong work ethic.

ReWorking Expert Advice

Flex Time

Lisa Mark is a partner in FlexTime Solutions, Inc., a northern New Jersey–based recruiting firm that offers flexible employment choices for marketing and communications professionals (*www.flextimesolutions.com*). The firm started in 1996, seeking to serve the needs of mid-career professionals who wanted flexibility to accommodate family or personal needs, as well as more senior professionals who have been downsized or want to get off the corporate fast track.

Today, FlexTime Solutions has a solid client list of Fortune 500 companies that take advantage of the firm's corps of experienced professionals for full-time, part-time, long-term, or short-term consulting assignments.

As the boomers gray, and as corporations continue to be leaner, executive placement specialists such as FlexTime Solutions are finding that an increasing number of their candidates are in the over-fifty category. Lisa Mark advises that, for older candidates, the key to a successful new career in consulting and flexible employment is to re-evaluate skills separately from your existing job. Think of yourself as portable hire, a portable executive, for example, who has the perfect skill set for the job at hand.

Those older than fifty should take full notice of Lisa Mark's empirical and practical suggestions for their job search as she answered our questions.

Q. *Do you see an increase in the over-fifty worker applying for positions?*

A. We see a continuation of the trend of companies downsizing or moving jobs overseas. At the same time, many older executives are seeking to make a career change in order to create a more flexible personal lifestyle for themselves. It is a function of the market and demographics.

Q. *Which kind of older professionals have been easier to place?*

A. We have been most successful placing those candidates who are flexible and able to adapt to different environments and work situations. Confidence, a proactive "get the job done" approach, and independent thinking are key attributes of the successful older professional. We find that the best candidates are willing to use whatever skills the client needs for the job without letting their egos get in the way.

Q. *Why are companies seeking out older employees?*

A. Many firms search for an older, more experienced professional for consulting assignments because they know that these workers have the proven ability to perform the specific tasks required. These companies know that they get a big bang for their buck with older executives—experience and know-how that are hard to find in younger professionals.

And, while usually the over-fifty-year-old candidate is not actively recruited for mid-level permanent slots, these candidates are often the first choice when converting temporary employees to permanent staff. As consultants, the older executive often becomes an invaluable member of the team, and younger managers feel more comfortable and less threatened with having them on staff permanently.

Q. *What are some resume tips for the older candidate?*

A. Over-fifty candidates need to repackage their many years of experience to meet the specific requirements of the job for which they are applying. This means promoting specific skills in a separate section, and highlighting those accomplishments that relate to the targeted job opening.

It is helpful to include your computer skills to overcome any possible doubts about your technological knowledge. Also, it has become acceptable to eliminate the dates of college graduation to avoid age discrimination. Under certain circumstances, you can even restate your job titles for past positions, if they aren't directly applicable to your targeted job opening. For example, if you did writing as part of your job as "Communications Director," you could change your title on the resume to "Senior Writer, Communications Department," if you are marketing yourself for a writing position versus a management position.

Q. *Can the older executive request work in more flexible assignments?*

A. Many professionals in mid- and upper-level careers are finding it easier to arrange telecommuting or shortened weeks. It is really a function of the marketplace and the comfort level of the supervisor.

Key advice for the over-fifty professional is to have a fully functioning home office set up. This means computer, cable or DSL Internet service, e-mail, fax machine, and perhaps a second phone line. If you are set up to work efficiently at home, you offer a strong measure of flexibility to your current or future employers. If you can be readily available and complete work in a timely manner, it fosters confidence in a work-from-home arrangement.

Q. *What about "job share" for the older worker?*

A. Our history indicates that, while it can be done, job sharing is not viable in most corporate settings. When it is successful, the two professionals are usually already in similar jobs at the same company. Critical to success are complementary working styles, a collaborative work ethic, and the strong desire to make the arrangement work. Having a supervisor who supports this arrangement is essential.

Another important factor in the job-share arrangement is the issue of "headcount." Most companies count each employee as one "headcount" per job. Two part-time workers will thus count as two "headcounts" for one job, and this may be a strong disincentive to authorize a job share arrangement.

Q. *What are the primary errors that older professionals make when interviewing?*

A. The older candidate faces some special challenges when interviewing for a new position. Most have had long careers spanning a variety of positions and responsibilities. It is very easy to fall into the trap of offering the interviewer too much information about your skills and experience. A better approach is to focus on the specific skills that are important to the position for which you are interviewing. Pull out accomplishments from your background that relate directly to the job, and focus on these rather than cataloguing your entire resume.

When it comes to discussing why you are seeking a new position or change of career direction, have good, solid reasons—and deliver them without apology. If you are seeking a change to a consulting assignment after working in staff positions your entire career, you should be able to explain these career motivation goals. Most hiring managers are now aware that careers change over time and that the position you once held may no longer be appealing to you for a variety of reasons.

Older candidates also need to present themselves as energetic, vital, and interested in the work world. Listen carefully to the interviewer, and tailor your responses to his or her line of conversation. Try to demonstrate that you are flexible and willing to adapt to new environments and new ways of doing things.

Sometimes older professionals are a bit uncomfortable with their own aging and where they now fit in the corporate environment. However, it is very important to refrain from making "age-related" comments, even if the interviewer appears to be your own age. You do not want to focus on age as a factor or to be identified as someone who is out of the mainstream with other professionals. Avoid comments like these:

- ✔ "Sorry, but I can't see a thing without my glasses!"
- ✔ "I'm really tired of long commutes and I'm looking to work from home."
- ✔ "My wife and I are buying a retirement home in Florida and I'm just looking for something to do until we move there in a couple of years."
- ✔ "Oh, I like to deal with people on the phone. I still can't figure out how to use e-mail."
- ✔ "I only want to take this job if you can give me less than full-time hours."

Any one of these comments will brand you as an "over the hill" worker who doesn't have a grasp of current corporate culture.

Q. *What about older professionals seeking benefits?*

A. Our experience shows that the over-fifty-year-old workers are definitely interested in getting the highest compensation they can for their services. Benefits are an important part of that compensation. This is one of the reasons that FlexTime Solution offers a range of benefits for its employees. While the benefits vary based on the number of hours worked, all employees who work more than twenty-five hours per week are offered both medical and dental plan options, long-term disability coverage, and paid vacation time. Holiday pay is usually included for those who work a full-time schedule, if the company participates in this program. As health-care costs continue to rise, our group health-care coverage becomes increasingly important to people over fifty, for whom individual insurance coverage can be extremely costly.

Q. *What are specific mistakes the over-fifty worker may make on the job?*

A. Professionals who have seasoned careers (over twenty-five years in the work force) are sometimes inflexible regarding their approach to an assignment. They believe that the way they have done things in the past is the best way to do it. This is a particular problem when encountering new work environments where flexibility in adapting new work habits is critical to success.

Some older workers also have a "know it all" attitude, which can be threatening to younger supervisors. They need to remember that their job as a consultant or new employee is to bring their wealth of experience to the table, to interact effectively with their coworkers, and to add value to the company. That's why they were hired!

Another mistake that older professionals make is not keeping current with technology. The vast majority of companies today use standard computer software packages in their everyday operations. It is essential that older workers know how to use word processing software, e-mail, the Internet, and spreadsheet or presentation software if it relates to their job function.

For example, most managers now use e-mail as a key means of communication for both formal and informal matters. If you want to give someone a written document, you need to send it by e-mail—not fax, mail, or hand delivery unless it was specifically requested as such.

One important note: Social mores change over time, and comments that were once commonplace on the job are no longer acceptable. Comments or actions that are construed as harassment (sexual or otherwise) will now result in dismissal instead of a "chat with the boss." In addition, misuse of the Internet (gambling, viewing sexually explicit matter, blogging, or even shopping) is now cause for dismissal as well.

Q. *What kinds of companies seek out the over-fifty employee?*

A. Smart, savvy companies are recognizing the employment trend of baby boomers leaving the work force. This loss will create a "brain drain," as older workers take proprietary knowledge of the company's history and systems with them as they go. As this trend becomes more apparent in the workplace, companies will seek to bring back former employees who have the proven skills they need.

Under these circumstances, the companies may be willing to offer such flexibility as part-time work, telecommuting, or compressed workweeks. Corporate culture is slowly starting to shift toward the retention of older workers instead of automatic retirement. Of course, it depends on the forward thinking of upper management, human resources, and individual managers, but hiring older workers in the future will be a necessity, not a choice.

When Continuing to Work is the Only Option

After you have completed the financial budgets analysis, is it evident that you will have to work into retirement? If yes, then you know that work and only work will make up the difference between what is needed to live and other sources of income.

Additionally, some long-term workers will be forced out of jobs years before they anticipated. Some will receive monetary buyouts while others will not. In either case, the income stream and medical benefits will end earlier than expected. How can people who find themselves in this pickle look for and find other work? Will they find comparable jobs with similar income?

The ReWorked Life

Sales Manager to General Manager

Angelo Sinisi had worked in the heating and boiler industry for thirty-seven years, rising to become the sales manager of a western Massachusetts company, located a short drive from his home and small sculpture studio.

At age sixty, he thought this position would be the last one, the final job to end a long and successful career, the job he anticipated would take him to retirement. Then, a management shakeup left him unemployed and still in need of income.

He found a consulting position with two different sales representative companies on Long Island, New York, on a commission-only basis and without any pension or medical benefits. Often he had to make the long drive from his home in Massachusetts. He decided to draw down social security at age sixty-two to make up the income difference between the lower income from consulting and the basic costs to live.

But Sinisi had kept up his network within the boiler industry and was contacted by the Bradford White Company in Ambler, Pennsylvania, manufacturers of water heaters. They hired him to assist their entrance into the boiler industry. As a result, the company purchased the Laars Corporation in Rochester, New Hampshire.

Bradford White offered Sinisi the Laars general manager's position, which he readily accepted. The package included salary, medical, and pension benefits. The only downside was that he and his wife had to move to Rochester. He left sculpting for the occasional weekend back in his Massachusetts home.

Sinisi, at age sixty-eight, is working full time at a job he enjoys and plans to continue working for a long time.

The Vanishing Pension Safety Net

Many current seniors regard their company's pension plan as the long-awaited source of promised income for the future. Yet, the hard reality is that some of these pensions may not be available upon retirement.

Take the case of the pilots at Delta Airlines. The airline company filed for bankruptcy and petitioned the Pension Benefit Guaranty Corporation (PBGC), informing this federal agency that it could no longer fund the pension plan for its pilots. In an instant, all of those men who had flown for the airline for years would collect a measly five cents on the dollar if that.

In one day, the lives of Delta's pilots changed forever for the worse because the money they had counted on for retirement was no longer available. How can these trained professionals, many over sixty, recoup the pension money they had counted on? The sad but honest answer is that they will never be able to find the replacement funds.

There is no way today to know if a company will declare bankruptcy at some point in the future, the main and only legal means to cancel a pension fund. The courts have decided that it is more advantageous for a company to restructure without debt than to force it to honor commitments to employees. That leaves the retiree out in the cold and out of luck.

401(k) Retirement Funds

Future retirees should also factor in the current worth of their company's 401(k) funds. The 401(k) remains one of the most common ways for individuals to invest for retirement. But, as Enron employees discovered, it is not necessarily the best. Sixty-two percent of their retirement contributions—$1.3 billion—was, by their own choice, invested in Enron stock. When Enron shares plummeted to less than one dollar, the anticipated funds evaporated. (Admittedly, this is an aberrant example. Enron employees believed their 401(k) plans would balloon into millions by keeping all funds in the company stock and not diversifying.) What would happen to your retirement plans if 62 percent of your total investment disappeared, never to return? It is better to diversify with assistance from a financial planner.

* * *

A Final Note

Many people will not be compelled by finances to work in retirement. But they still might want to. The question then becomes, what would they enjoy? If you are in this safe and good place, how do you decide what to do? What magazines do you buy? What television shows interest you? Are these signposts to a possible new vocation?

A television commercial for financial retirement shows a person who says, "I wanted to chase the dream before it became too late." What dream do you have? Can you answer the following?

✔ What are your skills?
✔ What are your main interests?
✔ Is there something you always wanted to do if you had the time?

Many stories in this book are about people who went on "to chase that dream," to volunteer, or to begin part-time or full-time second careers.

What do you want to do for the rest of your life?

4 First Steps on the Road to Work

"If you do not vote for yourself, do not expect others to vote for you."

—Moses Maimonides

The right frame of mind is key when embarking on a new job search. Consider the pursuit of employment the beginning of a brand new chapter in your life. Though looking for a job can be tedious, you must remain confident that you will find a job that will provide the amount of income you need and fulfill other social needs. Above all, you must be confident that the outcome of the search will be favorable.

A good outcome requires careful step-by-step preplanning to ensure that you get off to the right start. A well-thought-out plan can prevent missteps and the need to do it a second time.

A job search takes time, but you must remember that your time is not the primary consideration of the future employer or the marketplace. You may be anxious to begin some new job or trade, but it won't happen overnight. The process, from first contact to interview to callback to filling out forms, could take weeks—even months—to complete. The full-time work you seek may require a job search of anywhere from three to seven months.

Remember, also, that the job you did in the past—no matter how high you rose on the ladder of success in your job or occupation—may not be the skill set that will interest a new employer. For example, assume that for thirty years or more you worked as the Executive Vice President of Finance of a midsize company. If you now seek to work at Home Depot or Lowe's as an on-the-floor expert in carpentry and cabinetry (your hobby for forty years), the details and rigor of your prior professional financial background is of ancillary interest to the prospective employer—and may make them question whether your expectations for the current job are reasonable.

The ReWorked Life

Art Director to Newspaper Publisher

Royal Bruce Montgomery worked thirty-five years in advertising on Madison Avenue. He had been an art director, television producer, and creative director for large advertising agencies. He retired three times from the ad business, lured back again and again by the creative challenge and the money.

Years earlier in 1975, he and his wife purchased a summer home on Block Island, a small island off Rhode Island. In 1999, the couple retired permanently to Block Island. Montgomery purchased the *Block Island Times* newspaper, in which he saw an opportunity to draw wry cartoons and become immersed in the new island home.

The paper had been hampered by a lack of investment from its mainland owner and had never become more than a summer handout. Montgomery believed he could make it into a daily newspaper with a distinct voice and a mission. He used his big-business management skills, insisting that the new version of the paper had to grow by expanding the advertising base, improving the typography and design, and enlarging the scope and the purpose of the editorial page.

The revitalized *Block Island Times* eventually won many awards from the New England Press Association. Although some residents did not agree with many of the editorials, they were pleased that Montgomery had made it an energetic small newspaper for the small island (1,100 full-time residents).

In 2005, Montgomery sold the paper to other long-time Block Island residents with publishing experience, but he continues to work daily on the paper doing ads, cartoons, and bird columns. He also authored the humorous cartoon book, *Where the Hell Is Block Island?*

Step One: How Much Should You Work?

At the outset, there are basically two choices in your search for work: part time—now being referred to as flexible time—or full time. Once you have decided which one you want, this choice will direct your search efforts.

The existing positions will be advertised in newspaper classified ads and on bulletin boards or on the Internet as "Part time" or abbreviated "Pt. Time" or "PT." The term "part time" has no legally defined hours, but generally it means twenty hours or less per week. (Many positions are part time so that employers will not have to provide benefits.)

Full-time work will commit you to a minimum of a thirty-five hour week. Is this what you had in mind when considering changing occupations? Or did you want to gradually scale down your work time? If you answered yes to the latter, full-time work is not for you.

A frequent gripe heard from people who have changed to a less stressful job is that they didn't expect full-time work in such an environment to include the usual nine-to-five workplace problems. If you need income, you will have to work the maximum number of hours that you can. However, full-time work may represent a bigger commitment or more stress than you anticipated.

Step Two: Self-Assessment

The first step is to evaluate your personal interests. If you want to find a job that is significantly different from what you've done all your life, it will be helpful to rate your preferences and see how these match up with your existing talents.

If you have been harboring a lifelong yearning to do some activity—teach, work with your hands, be in business for yourself, work outdoors, etc.—now is the time to list these choices. In some cases, you may need on-the-job training, schooling, or certification to accomplish the goal.

Fill in these answers. "The types of work I would most like to do are:" (First choice. Second choice. Third choice.)

1. _____
2. _____
3. _____

Do these choices look as if they will supply the income you need? Are these choices practical ones, matching the skills and experience you possess?

Work Interest Checklist

Compose a checklist of different variables to clearly see what interests you and what does not. Here is a list of some common selections.

1. Full-time / Part-time
2. Indoors / Outdoors
3. With people / Work alone
4. Morning / Afternoon / Evening
5. Money important / Money not a concern
6. In my field / Something different
7. I've always dreamed of doing?
8. My feelings about stress are
9. What does my spouse think I'd be good at?
10. What do others perceive I could do?

The ReWorked Life

Investment Banker to Coach to COO

Sam Marrone graduated from the Naval Academy at Annapolis and later served as a Marine infantry platoon commander in Vietnam. When he returned from military service, he started an investment banking career in New York City.

In 1987, he worked for Barclays Bank PLC, heading its initial entry into buying and selling U.S. government securities. The venture's success led Barclays to move him to its London headquarters, where he became CEO of the bank's Markets Division. The clash of national cultures resulted in him losing the job. Many Americans lose out on jobs that move overseas; Marrone lost his job when he, not it, moved overseas.

After returning to the United States, he became the Executive Vice President of ABN AMRO, North America He continued for a few years with the overseas bank, then retired at age fifty-eight.

Marrone then became coach of rugby and freshman football at Fairfield Prep in Connecticut. For many years high school coaching had been his dream retirement job, but soon he realized that the workday did not begin until 3:30 P.M. He had too much free time on his hands.

A close friend had started a small manufacturing company that dealt exclusively in military sales worldwide. The start-up company required additional capital and, more importantly, a savvy executive who understood the military culture. Marrone was doubly qualified to become the new COO.

Today, Marrone is part of a management team that has doubled the growing company's revenues. Manufacturing has been a tonic, both challenging and stimulating. Ironically, his career started and will end with the military.

Step Three: Skill Set Assessment

It is one thing to list your dream job, another to be frank about whether you possess the talent to do it. On the other hand, if you are looking in the same field of expertise, you already have the qualifications to look in a similar area.

In a *Seinfeld* episode, the recently laid-off George contemplates his dream job and suggests, "Sports announcer." Jerry asks what qualifications his friend has to do this job and George replies, "I like sports."

Too often, people demonstrate naiveté when it comes to finding a new job for which they have minimal skills. This lack does not have to halt your search, but it should throw up caution flags and force more introspection. The thought process should be:

✔ How can I be trained for the new assignment?
✔ How long a learning curve is there?
✔ Will it be worthwhile monetarily?
✔ In the final analysis, is it feasible?

Step Four: Skill Matching

The next exercise is to match work that you want to do with the skills that you have. Use a separate sheet of paper for each job.

Job Assessment (example)

Job: Customer Service Representative—Telephone

Job Description: Answer consumer calls relating to ordering new merchandise, status of past orders, payment issues, shipping information, and all other questions and problems, including complaints. (Rate your skills H for High, M for Medium, and L for Low.)

Required Skills	*Your skills assessment*
Pleasant phone voice	
Patience	
Problem solving	
Dealing with abusive callers	

Step Five: Announcement

The last step to finding a new job is to announce this intention to friends, associates, and family. Telling your network that you're looking for work will increase the number of potential sources for the search. Statistics indicate that your network will probably be the source of your next job.

It is vital to be specific about what you are looking for and how much time you want to devote to this new venture. A personal phone call is the best way to indicate your new work intentions. E-mail is the next best option, allowing you to reach a great number of people in one move. Additionally, friends or associates on the e-mail list can also forward your request to their appropriate e-mail contacts.

Here are some useful sample look-for-work-announcements taken from people we interviewed for the book but with their names changed:

"Hi, friends, it is Tom Micks. I left the job at Acme Corporation, and now I'm looking for part-time work, preferably doing sports coaching for kids mornings or afternoons. Contact me by return e-mail or this telephone number. Thank you."

"Evelyn Molina has completed training as a licensed manicurist and is looking to offer this service to nursing home or assisted living facilities. Many thanks for any help you can provide. Rates reasonable."

From: Frank Finland. "I was laid off last week. My job has moved to India. I seek full-time employment. For thirty-two years, I was a VP supervisor of Customer Service. I am also interested in changing careers. All leads appreciated. Respond by e-mail or telephone. Heartfelt appreciation."

The ReWorked Life

Owner to Salesperson

Richard D. Lewis had started out in the family's printing business in his early twenties as a salesperson making cold calls. In the competitive printing trade, new accounts represented the lifeblood of the business.

When Lewis's father retired thirty years ago, he assumed the responsibility of running the business alone. In addition to the sales duties, Lewis was now fully in charge of the management of the pressroom, working closely with the bookkeeper and the accountant, and doing the hiring and firing of personnel.

Every small business comes with its own degrees of stress, and the printing business was no exception, especially in the highly detailed quality cosmetic industry printing work of Lewis's firm. Every job had to be error free, and delivered on time.

Approaching age sixty-five, Lewis had to make a decision about the business. The firm's sole assets were the printing presses and the 12,500 square feet of floor space in the building that the company had owned since 1982. He wondered what he would do if he closed the printing business.

He finally decided to sell the floor and the printing presses and take a sales job with another printing company to bookend his career in sales. The sales-only job reduced any management responsibilities and almost eliminated the negative stress.

Today, Lewis is out of the office daily, calling on old and new accounts. All the other chores are the new firm's concern. At sixty-seven, Lewis can concentrate solely on sales.

Each request clarified the intent of the search. Notice that each indicated a specific way (e-mail or telephone) for the reader to respond. All solicitations were brief and informative. There's no need to pour out feelings or emotions. Your network understands the reasons for your hunt for work. Writing less is the smart tip when composing these search requests.

ReWorking Expert Advice

Health Insurance

People anticipating new assignments or currently staying at work have to navigate health insurance choices that often seem like a maze with too many turns and too many exits. But this is an important consideration for people who are retiring or retirees looking to return to work.

In this instance, we relied upon not one specialist but the consensus of several health insurance professionals who have studied the disparate and perplexing choices that exist for you before you become eligible for Medicare at age sixty-five. Please note that the matter of your own health coverage should be more fully researched than any cursory information or helpful hints that are cited on these pages. We strongly recommend that you undergo a thorough examination of different plans and costs with a health insurance professional.

As an older worker, you face significant medical coverage choices if:

✔ You are laid off or fired.
✔ You take early retirement.
✔ The company/organization reneges on continuing paying for your health insurance.
✔ You must pay for your own health insurance until you are eligible for Medicare.

Here are the main questions posed to the health professionals:

Q. *How soon before individuals reach sixty-five years should they consider and study the various Medicare options?*

A. A person should begin investigating Medicare and ancillary options at least six months before turning sixty-five. The first place to check is Social Security by telephoning 1-800-MEDICARE. You can also learn more about Medicare by going online at *www .medicare.gov* or *www.ssa.gov* and requesting printed material be sent to your home. Or you can pick up the many booklets and bulletins about social security and Medicare at your local office.

Q. *Is there an informative and easy-to-read Web site that can explain the ins and outs of the new Medicare, particularly Part D, the pre-scription drug benefits?*

A. Yes, Walgreen's Pharmacy maintains an informative Web site at *www.walgreens.com.* Click "Pharmacy," then in the left-hand column, in the third section down, click "Medicare Facts." This will bring up a series of brief descriptions of all the different Medi-care options, including basic explanations of Medicare Parts A, B, C, and, importantly, Part D—Prescription Drug Benefits.

Farther down this page, you will find additional information that answers many more questions and concerns. (Two additional Web sites are AARP at *www.AARP.org* and the National Academy of Elder Law Attorneys at *www.naela.org.*)

Q. *Some people choose to buy a supplemental Medicare Plan B from private insurance companies. Why?*

A. Let's review first how Plan B works: In 2007, you will have to pay around $100 a month for this plan. (The annual increase in premiums is decided and posted every year in the fall on the Social Security Web site under "Cost of Living.") But there are certain payments and coverage gaps in the government's Plan B that it will not pay for, so many seniors choose to add on supplemental plans.

These are generally referred to as Medigap policies and are sold by private insurance companies to pay for some of the items that the basic Medicare Plan B does not cover, such as deductibles and coinsurance. There are ten specific standardized plans designated Plans A through Plan J. All of these other supplemental plans will cost more per month for added benefits.

Q. *How does one find these supplemental Plan B options?*

A. There are hundreds of providers who offer these Plan B supplemental policies, including the major insurers such as Blue Cross and Blue Shield, United Health Care, Cigna, and many other smaller and regional companies.

But before you begin the search, we suggest you contact your state insurance department by telephone or online. You will discover Medicare Plan B information and probably a list of those private insurance companies within the state that offer these supplemental plans. Of note is that the monthly fees for Plan B often vary by county from private insurers within the state.

Q. *What happens if I lose access to medical insurance after being laid off by my company?*

A. In 1986, the government passed COBRA (Consolidated Omnibus Budget Reconciliation Act), a continuation of group health plans for employers with twenty or more employees. Usually the coverage duration is eighteen months for employees who are covered under the group plan. The terminated employee picks up the total cost of whatever health insurance plans the companies offer. (Many states have their own continuation rules for group health insurance plans for those companies with less than twenty employees.)

Q. *If I am forced into COBRA, do I have to continue the expensive out-of-network physician coverage? Or can I switch to a less expensive in-network plan?*

A. Most group health insurance plans that have more than one plan allow terminated employees to change plans at the renewal date of the policy (commonly referred to as open enrollment). But remember that at the end of the year-and-a-half coverage, you are no longer eligible to continue with the company's group coverage. Then, you are on your own.

Q. *I took early retirement, I'm sixty years old, and my company will not pay for health insurance. How do I find out about health insurance to bridge the five-year period before I start Medicare?*

A. We recommend you first contact the state insurance department. There you should find a list of all the private insurance carriers within the state. New York also had created a policy called "Healthy New York," which offers HMO coverage for its citizens, a low-cost plan that may be offered by other states as well.

Q. *I am on Medicare Plans A and B. Suppose I am hired full time by a company. Will its plan replace my Medicare coverage?*

A. Most likely the new company plan will act as the "primary" insurer, with Medicare being the "secondary" insurer. (This assumes your new company has more than twenty employees.) Of course, retaining Medicare B as a secondary carrier may become expensive. However, we concur that you never want to quit the Medicare Plan B because if you drop it, there will be a penalty charge if and when you want to pick it up again.

Q. *If I go into business for myself and fill out Schedule C, can I deduct the costs of Medicare Plan B, the other supplemental payments to Plan B, and the Plan D Prescription Drug Benefits, as a business expense?*

A. No.

Q. *Do you see any relief ahead from the high cost of health care?*

A. The cost of the delivery of medical care today escalates annually at a staggering rate and will continue to do so unless the federal government intercedes.

✳ ✳ ✳

A Final Note

It is very important to maintain a concise list of the outcomes from the solicitations and inquiries about work. The list should record whom you contacted, their response, and names of other people to contact. Send a thank-you to everyone who assisted in the search. Having completed all the recommended exercises, you are well on your way to finding new work.

5 The Psychology of Searching for Work

"A lot . . . nowadays have a B.A., M.D., or Ph.D. Unfortunately, they do not have a J.O.B."

—Antoine "Fats" Domino

Looking for work requires a clear rethinking of goals and objectives. Changes in life's circumstances—financial, social, and health-related—will dictate when and how you look for employment.

Experts recommend a transitional period to move you from full-time work in a career to some other type of employment setting. Today, more and more companies and organizations have implemented some type of interim work program. These measures will increase over time as more people in the nation's work force turn fifty years old and start to consider other work-related retirement options.

Three functional issues determine how you pursue finding other work: determination, preference, and control.

Determination: Resolve to undergo the search for something new, to cooperate fully with the marketplace's demand for the customary job application and job interview formats.

Preference: Choose either a personal interest to pursue regardless of the income generation, or opt for the kind of work that will meet your expense requirements.

Control: Decide where, when, and for how long you'll continue in the new work situation.

How to Exit the Career

How you exit the lifelong job represents an important step in the decision to transition from a full-time, life-defining career into a newer type of work. Essentially, your leaving is either voluntary or involuntary as a result of an early retirement offer, health reasons, job disappearance due to economic factors, or mandatory age retirement. It is often a situation of pull or push.

In the voluntary example, a worker has probably made a short-term plan after having calculated income and expenses to determine how and when to retire. In the involuntary or forced case, control over the decision has been taken away, and the terminated employee suddenly has to face a daunting decision, whether to continue to look for similar work at approximate pay levels or to search for something different.

The worker who makes the deliberate decision to retire is in a better mental state to address all aspects of retirement, including what to do next on the subject of work (with the exception of health-related conditions forcing people into too-early retirement). We found no one who had voluntarily left a career who had not done careful planning for the move. Frequently, though not always, they had a well-thought-out retirement plan to put into action. Not all these preplanned strategies reached fruition, however, and some retirees discovered that they had been naive or unrealistic about expectations for the future in retirement.

Many people in their mid-fifties have been unexpectedly hit by the sudden thud of dismissal, which combines negative feelings of rejection and disappointment. Psychologically, these workers are forced to confront the reality that they are expendable after having given most of their lives to the company or organization. Disillusionment and bitterness soon transform into anger.

The ReWorked Life

Human Resources to Salesman

When Bob Moore turned fifty-five, his company, Northrop Aviation in California, offered him early retirement with an extra two-year bonus payout. He had suffered two bypass heart surgeries and wanted to avoid the stress of returning to HR part time or even consulting in the same field.

He felt too young to do nothing in retirement. His son, along with some partners, had started a small software consulting company, which had perfected a unique computer scheduling system for public and private blood donor organizations. Moore offered to become the company's chief salesperson for this product.

He learned the details of the software and, more important, how to demonstrate it on the computer, significantly increasing his technical skills. He identified the target market segments of the blood donation markets and started cold calling. To his surprise, he found the activity stimulating and different from the mental challenges and multi-committee activities of human resources. He also liked being on his own.

Moore understood that if prospective buyers saw the product firsthand, this increased the probability of sales. He regularly made the rounds of the blood equipment trade shows. The new travel and interaction with people proved motivating.

Over the five years he worked for the company, technological changes made it possible to set up a sales office at home. But Moore could not make the transition to a home office. All his working life, he had put on a suit and tie and driven to the workplace, and this is what he continued to do. Eventually, he permanently retired after a second and successful career as a salesman.

These are a sampling of a few comments we heard from seniors abruptly terminated.

✔ "The Department gathered in the conference room. I thought it was a birthday party. Then the head of HR told us we were all let go. The recent merger with a larger company had duplicated our functions. I had worked there for thirty-seven years, and I was gone in fifteen minutes."

✔ "Management had assured us for years that even though the technology had gradually moved overseas, our U.S. plant was productive and profitable. Then the factory closed, and we all received a pink slip."

✔ "The CEO said our dismissal was a necessary downsizing. He explained further that it was not personal, it was just a redeployment or destaffing, a right-sizing—and work-force reduction, he also called it. I came up with few additional euphemisms: an expedited management triage, a selective job partition, and, my favorite, an occupational fumigation. But the truth was that at age fifty-three, I had been punched a one-way ticket to unemployment's Palookaville."

The problem with the unforeseen guillotine of termination late in a person's career is that it upsets the plans for retirement. In addition, medical payments may not be continued and the worker will have to pay the COBRA costs out of pocket. Finally, payments into the pension or defined contribution plan will end.

Further, perhaps the spouse continues to work, and this is an additional psychological challenge. The person at home feels unproductive. If unemployment continues for a long time, it will alter retirement plans.

But the most dangerous and stressful feeling that older workers often suffer is a lack of confidence that they can find comparable jobs quickly in the same career. The specter of unemployment with the resulting depletion of savings or retirement funds dangles like the proverbial sword of Damocles over their uncertain futures.

We cite these somber events because they occur every day in America. But for the laid-off senior, rather than an emotional tailspin the unexpected termination provides an opportunity to rethink work, refigure retirement, and reinvent herself in another job.

Who Needs to Work

It is useful to list the income sources that motivate people to consider work in later years. There are three categories:

Social security only—This group will have to work full-time to make up the difference between the monthly social security income and the total costs of living.

Some retirement income and social security—Many in this category will experience a gap (large or small) between income and expenses. They can opt for full-time work to generate an overage of income, or choose part-time employment to close the gap between income and expenses.

Adequate income not to work again—These seniors can opt for volunteer positions, work at hobbies, or even enjoy indulgences depending upon the amount of wealth they have accumulated.

Too many workers say, "When I retire, my 401(k) or IRA or my pension contribution will be worth 'X' dollars." Yet changes in the economy, particularly the stock market, can have a major impact on the amount that will actually be available for retirement.

The ReWorked Life

PR Manager to Book Writer

As a young boy, Rudy Marzano became a loyal Brooklyn Dodgers fan after watching a Dodgers-Giants game in 1934 at Ebbets Field. The pitcher for the Bums that day was Walter "Boom Boom" Beck, who allegedly was given the nickname because his pitches resulted in "boom off the bat" or "boom off the wall." The raucous Brooklyn crowd would chant, "Boom! Boom!" to welcome him.

It would take more than sixty years and full retirement to reawaken Marzano's pleasure and interest in those wonderful Brooklyn Dodgers teams of his youth.

After graduating from Rutgers, in 1951, Marzano began a career in journalism at the *Newark Evening News*. He did general assignments and covered county politics. But in the early 1960s he saw that the newspaper could not survive (it closed in 1972 after its first strike) and changed jobs, eventually working in public relations at AT&T in downtown Manhattan.

At age fifty-nine, Marzano voluntarily checked out of the Bell System with a bonus package and all his benefits. He was offered but refused similar positions with other companies as well as a county post in Essex, New Jersey.

The afternoons started to hang heavy, and he wondered how he could fill in the time. He decided to return to his writing career and to an interest that had never flagged: the Dodgers. Marzano's book, *The Brooklyn Dodgers in the 1940s: How Robinson, MacPhail, Reiser and Rickey Changed Baseball*, was published by McFarland and Company to great acclaim.

He has written a sequel entitled *The Last Years of the Brooklyn Dodgers*, which will come out in 2007.

Transition from Career to New Work

One of the most important learning experiences for you is to find a healthy transitional approach from full retirement into part-time work or back to full-time employment in another undertaking. You need the opportunity to seek choices.

There are numerous stories in the media and from our own research of someone retiring on Friday and waking up on Monday with a horrible sense of loneliness, unable to adapt quickly to not working. We recommend a bridge job if you can find it. The ideal place to find this flexible kind of work is with your current firm or organization. The company where you have been working for a long time knows and values your experience, and this asset promotes the best possible chance of negotiating shorter or fewer workdays. It is also important to remember that with the reduction of hours comes a lessening of responsibility and, possibly, a lowering of self-esteem. Another valuable reason for seeking out a bridge job is the empowerment it will provide you, allowing you to dictate terms for retirement.

ReWorking Expert Advice

Transitioning Out of Your Company

Bob Moore served as an Executive Vice President of Human Resources, spending twenty-five years counseling many would-be retirees about early retirement, company buyouts, and other work-related questions from both blue-collar and white-collar employees.

He is a firm believer in pragmatism and reality when it comes to thinking about leaving your company before the official time for retirement. His counsel: "There's an old saying that goes, 'Don't give up dirty water until you have clean.' This is applicable to those over fifty who wonder whether to remain with the company or to leave early. It is always smart to have a plan on the back burner."

Anxiety or concern about income, medical benefits, and quality of life will induce or compel many older than fifty years old to consider staying on the job. However, some employees may not want to wait until turning sixty or sixty-five and instead will consider the possibilities of exiting early by making a transitional move.

The stay-or-leave decision will be one of the most important and difficult. Once you exit a company permanently, the probability of returning in the same position and at the same salary are practically nil. There are many strategies and considerations for you to consider before making the ultimate decision to stay or go.

Bob Moore provided the questions seniors must ask about flexible time and early retirement. He also gave answers for some of the real-world aspects of staying put or trying to negotiate an earlier time out.

Q. *What if the company needs you full time?*

A. If the company requires your services or skills on a full-time basis, it has no interest in either encouraging you to leave prematurely or allowing you to move to some part-time assignment.

Q. *How do pension systems work if there are flexible assignments?*

A. Retirement packages are either defined contribution (i.e., the amount of money an employee puts into a pension) or defined benefit, which is company funded, often on an average of the highest salary over a three- or five-year basis. In the case of the former, if an employee opts for flexible or lower hours per week at a significant diminution of salary, then there will be fewer dollars going into that person's retirement fund.

Q. *Can a person considering retirement ask for and receive confidentiality when discussing transitioning out with Human Resources?*

A. As a general rule the HR executive will keep conversations confidential, but if a highly valuable or indispensable person—one whom the company depends upon—floats an early-out work proposal, the HR person must inform higher management.

Q. *How can employees learn more about possible flexible work without visiting Human Resources?*

A. Companies that are innovative with transitional or flexible work schedule for the older employee will publicize these plans through company electronic bulletin boards. A good way is to listen for and learn about what happened to other employees who sought out these new retirement methods.

Q. *Who in the company is more likely to be granted flextime?*

A. A rule of thumb is that employees below the vice-president level might be more inclined to receive some part-time assignment. If two people meet the job description and the other person is over fifty and looking for a flexible work schedule, it makes the flextime request to management significantly easier to approve.

Q. *Assume an executive-level employee wants to work less in order to transition into retirement. What are the options?*

A. There are several options. The company may agree to hire you as a consultant without benefits. Or it will continue allowing you to work for a year or eighteen months with the main proviso that you train a replacement. Or conversely, the company could demand that you start to train someone else immediately and as soon as that person is up to speed, you'll be let go. Remember, all successful companies have succession contingencies in place for upper management.

Q. *Are there other general hints about asking for flexible time?*

A. Yes. How is the company doing? If revenues and profits are up, then management may feel more openhanded about allowing an early departure. But if the company is experiencing bad times and you are a valued employee with lots of knowledge, it will not want to add to its woes by letting you go.

Q. *What other variables about the company might affect requesting flexible time?*

A. Two factors: the company's location and the ready availability of replacement personnel. If the company is in a high-cost-of-living area such as New York or San Francisco, it may have difficulty attracting senior level people to take your job. Similarly, if the company is out in the boondocks, then it will not be so easy to tap into local management. These two extremes work to an employee's advantage when trying to negotiate a transitional time to leave.

Q. *What if an employee meets negative resistance from the company about early or transitional retirement?*

A. A safety play is to find out beforehand if you can consult part-time at the competition. This works if the competitor is either within normal driving range or you can establish a virtual office at home. But this is a last, and maybe a desperate, ploy that you want to avoid if at all possible.

Q. *What are your final thoughts on the flexible future for retirees?*

A. Companies will be forced to become innovative in how they deal with the newly turning fifty-year-olds. My father's generation stayed with the same company until age sixty-five and retired. Now opportunities and second-chance careers abound for you. Companies that want to retain the skill set and the experience of older workers have to find some way to retain them in the work force, even at fewer hours and decreased responsibility.

Less Work at the Same Job

Many professions, such as nursing, realize that older, practiced workers possess experience and skills but cannot maintain a rigorous thirty-five- or forty-hour week. So, companies and research organizations at universities are studying the ways to adjust work schedules to accommodate senior staffers.

In light of the media attention on boomers and their remaining in jobs longer, we predict that within the next three to five years, new feasibility studies will be implemented that address a major shift in retaining the seasoned senior in the same occupation. Management will find ways to allow flexible scheduling if it sees work smoothly flowing as before.

Using a Support Network

Looking for work remains one of life's more taxing endeavors. It is a process that's filled with daily rejection and subject to increased levels of stress. One good way to help reduce the anxiety is to develop a support group to help bolster you in the wearisome process.

One of the best methods we discovered to eliminate some of the strain was to search for work with a friend who is also looking for new employment. This is the proverbial buddy system, and it is an effective method of expediting success. It allows people to meet and to talk during the day about the search process. Importantly, both searchers should have an optimistic approach to the effort at hand.

The ReWorked Life

Supervisor to Coffee Entrepreneur

Gene Hicks worked in Ohio at NV Phillips (formerly Sylvania/ GTE) for thirty-nine years, starting as an hourly employee and working his way up to the position of quality manager. One upsetting aspect of the job was the horrible-tasting coffee the company served, resulting in half-empty pots and a full day's grumbling.

Hicks set out to discover what produced a delicious cup of coffee. After months of reading and research, he realized that four variables determined the optimum taste: beans, blends, roaster, and persistence toward perfection. He started to purchase high-quality coffee for home consumption and to treat coworkers at Phillips.

Hicks opted for early retirement at age fifty-five and headed to the woods of Ely, Minnesota, to begin his seasonal avocation as fishing guide. He decided to use his considerable coffee knowledge to sell his own line of gourmet coffees, specially ordered from a well-known master roaster.

At the outset, he gave away six-ounce plastic bags of his blends to the fishing customers. Some asked to buy the coffee in larger sizes. Later, the Silver Rapids Lodge in Ely began using his blends for its tourist clientele.

Encouraged by family and friends, he posted a Web site at *www.genehicks.com*. The mail-order-only coffees exude Hicks's passion for the best Arabica beans. Many feature woodsy names: Fishing, Good Morning, Campfire, and Canoe. The Fine Food and Beverage Federation awarded him its honor of "Finest coffee in America." Hicks's fame has been spread by word of mouth. Over the past year, sales have tripled, and he is now receiving inquiries about his product from up-scale supermarkets.

* * *

A Final Note

Another suggestion is to form your own board of directors, people who want to help you realize your re-employment goals. It works if you can have the board members assign you specific tasks and deadlines for the job search. Their constant inquiry about how things are going can be more productive than your own self-management. They should be encouraging and help keep you positive and goal-oriented.

6 | **Job Search**

> *"Find a job you like, and you add five days to every week."*
>
> —H. Jackson Browne Jr.

There are many places to look for a prospective job; thus, it is important to narrow the possible areas of exploration. Naturally we recommend prioritizing the places that will offer the greatest probability of success. We'll cover online searches in detail in the next chapter, but first we'll focus on other job search venues you may not have thought of.

The best way to find work is to stay with the job at hand, if you can tolerate it. The second-best option is to move your skills to a competitor. The third option is to reinvent yourself in a new job or occupation.

Staying with the Job at Hand

The current place of employment is the first place you should look. This may seem like simple-minded advice, but remaining in the current career at the same company or firm offers significant benefits.

The advantages are many, including continued income stream, medical benefits, ongoing pension contributions, and familiarity with the workplace and coworkers. In addition, if you opt to stay on the job, you will not experience the worry of where to find the next job.

However, there are many reasons why staying rooted in the current job may represent the wrong choice.

✔ Impending possibility of a permanent layoff
✔ Probability that the company will demand an early-retirement buyout soon
✔ Ending of pension plan
✔ Ending of free or paid-in medical benefits
✔ Company's/supervisor's knowledge that you are waiting to retire
✔ Constant stress
✔ Dissatisfaction with the work
✔ Ongoing diminution of responsibility
✔ Downgrading of your job
✔ Extensive travel to and from the job

Freelancing with the Same Company

Your current company, firm, or organization is the first and best place to try to negotiate a flexible schedule that will permit substantially fewer hours as you gravitate from paid employer to independent contractor.

Learn what has been company policy regarding flexible schedules for its employees. The chances are good that your proposal will succeed if part-time work or reduced hours per week have been granted to other employees. Point out that it will be less expensive for the company to keep you on a retainer or part-time basis than going through the rigorous and time-consuming task of finding a full-time replacement who is not familiar with the business.

List upcoming projects you can accomplish on reduced hours. Then discuss with your supervisor your desire to move toward retirement. Stress, however, that you would like to stay productive for the company on a project-by-project basis. Point out that there will be cost savings to the company, which will no longer have to pay social security payments and other expenses on your behalf.

We do not recommend attempting a reduced schedule with companies that have frowned on this type of arrangement in the past. Some firms are unyielding toward anyone in their work force who does not put in the standard five-day week.

Contacting the Competitor

Working for the competitor may seem like heresy but it has proved to be one of the most effective ways for you to achieve a flexible work schedule, particularly if your own company or organization cannot grant your request for less time.

This strategy succeeds best if one of the competitors is located in the same geographical area where you live, or at least within commuting distance. But in the world of work-at-home and Internet, it is also possible to find a reduced-time job with a competitor anywhere in the world.

Our advice is first to contact any person you know at the competing company. Be sure to send a resume along with a letter or e-mail. Follow up the request with a phone call.

The next step is to contact Human Resources at the competitor, inquiring directly if it offers consulting or independent contractor work. If you receive a positive reply, craft a constructive cover letter with attached resume that states the intention to look for reduced-time employment. It may also be helpful if you send a copy of the letter to someone within the competing company who knows your work and can vouch for it.

Contacting Suppliers or Purchasers of Your Company's Product or Service

These are also clever places to solicit employment opportunities, either full time or part time. Your company has purchased goods or service from suppliers in the past, and, at minimum, the suppliers will often interview you as a courtesy. The same applies to the purchasers of your company's product or service. They, too, will often welcome a meeting.

It may be a tangible benefit for these suppliers and purchasers to hire someone who knows the inside of a company with which they deal frequently. The key question they will ask is if you feel comfortable contacting former coworkers and supervisors.

The ReWorked Life

Software Exec to Internet Hat Success

For thirty years, Ernie DelMonico concentrated on expanding his banking software company, which numbered many of the nation's banks as customers. Yet always looming in the background—calling to him from the echoes of the family business—was the shop DelMonico Hatter in New Haven, Connecticut, opened in 1908.

Located across from the Yale University campus, DelMonico Hatter had barely survived the catastrophic decline in the fashion of men's hats and has remained the last haberdashery store in Connecticut. DelMonico Hatter had always kept a large and specialized hat and cap inventory and could offer hard-to-find styles to customers anywhere. But the days had long vanished of men wearing hats to work, to the baseball game, or to anywhere.

After retiring at age sixty-four, DelMonico had to make some decisions regarding the hat and cap store. He decided to launch an Internet Web site. Initially, while consumers first began to find the existence of this new site, there was no sales activity. Then, orders started to come in from around the country as people found this cap and hat company selling over the Internet.

A year later, the shop's sales business had increased significantly. DelMonico was startled at the success of the online sales. He made three important decisions: to launch a professionally designed Web site (*www.DelmonicoHatter.com*), to place an advertisement on Google listing the shop above the line, and to devote three full days a week to overseeing the business.

He joked, "All of my life I tried to avoid the hat business of my grandfather and father. But the Internet pulled me back in and I'm really enjoying selling hats all over the world. More important, I'm busy every week."

Trade Associations

Every trade or occupation maintains an organization, which is an excellent source of employment opportunities. Many of these have online employment areas for employers to list job openings as well as for members to post resumes.

Further, trade associations usually list major companies or organizations employing members, along with full mailing addresses, e-mail addresses, and telephone numbers for these companies or organizations. In addition, there is usually someone at the association whose job is to manage employment solicitations. It will be helpful to e-mail or telephone this person and clarify what kind of job you are searching for and what the best method is to pursue it.

Many trade groups also publish newsletters or hard-copy bulletins (in addition to monthly or quarterly online newsletters) that offer classified ads for job seekers free or at a nominal cost. Again, this kind of advertisement will only be useful if you make clear the kind of work you are seeking and the amount of time you want to devote to it.

Finally, publications and books abound listing companies and personnel. Many of these books can be found in the local public library or in college libraries. Note that many of these publications may be out of date; to obtain the most current data, use the Internet.

Sometimes it may not be easy to gain access to college libraries, but if you take an adult education course, this will qualify you for right of entry into the library and valuable and extensive job databases.

Trade Shows

If trade shows are scheduled in your city in or near where you live, this is also an opportunity for you to explore potential job openings. A show includes people in the same line of work and probably features an exhibition area filled with suppliers that sell to the industry. It's important to canvass both areas. Be sure to let associates know ahead of time if you are going to the show so they can provide you with a list of their network contacts.

Remember that the attendees of the show have come to promote their companies and services. They will not want to cede a lot of time to listen to any long-winded pitch by you for employment.

Narrow down the search to those companies and suppliers with whom you've experienced a personal relationship. You want to obtain a company contact name, an e-mail address, and any other information that could be valuable in applying for a part-time or full-time position.

Don't make the mistake of dropping off a business card and asking someone to deliver it to Human Resources or anyone else. Nothing will ever come of this request.

The University Alumni Association

Going back to college to check on possible job offerings is also a possibility. Many colleges and universities maintain job placement bulletin boards, available exclusively to alumni.

A smart tip also is to participate in free career assessment tests that many universities offer. (This is a new service that many graduates do not know exists.) This college testing will be especially helpful to those who want to experiment with some new vocation or business. We suggest a telephone conversation with someone in the college careers office to begin this process.

Your class secretary may have an up-to-date list of class members' e-mail addresses that could be sent to you. If you receive an annual class newsletter, it may have the e-mail addresses of class-mates, whom you can contact to indicate your new work search.

When it is time to contribute "What's new?" information for the next newsletter, you can write about your work quest, including your intent to do something different. Some of our friends began their search this way and specifically requested hints and advice from their classmates. The e-mails poured in from people who had experienced the same work/retirement situation with valuable tips on how to proceed (many are incorporated in this book).

The contacting and networking with classmates the same age offers a bonus if you are looking for work in a place where some of these alumni have already retired. This is true for any part-time or full-time employment and particularly useful for future volunteer work. These contacts can provide names and addresses of useful employment contacts and indicate where they'd recommend you not apply.

Printed Matter

Newspapers and magazines are the traditional method for companies and organizations to advertise available jobs. Be sure to read the classifieds in your local or community newspaper. In addition, there are Internet versions of these resources: classified ads on newspapers' Web sites; job listings and employment agency ads on job search Web sites and job boards, some geared to particular trades or industries; and the Career Opportunities pages of companies' own Web sites.

If you know someone at the advertising company, use that contact to find a back door so that your resume does not come in over the transom like everyone else's. Don't forget that there are hundreds, maybe thousands, of other people also reading these ads.

Use the *Pennysaver* and any other free newspapers as resources in your search. These usually contain some classified ads, though probably they will be less looked-at than the daily newspaper.

Community Bulletin Boards

The community in which you live also has a multitude of resources to aid your job search. Religious institutions, clubs or associations (e.g., Kiwanis, Rotary, etc.), and even the mayor's office or City Hall may have bulletin boards that allow you to post your job search request. The bulletin boards may also contain work postings.

You will need to type a brief request with a bold headline that states precisely what kind of work you're looking for and how many hours you are available. Put a telephone number where you can be contacted. Do not put only an e-mail address; the people who contact you will have many questions concerning your request and will want to speak to you. (Bring tacks, push pins, or tape with you.)

Canvassing the Local Retail Establishments

Every local retail establishment is a prospective employer. The AARP Web site lists leading American companies that have implemented programs to solicit and hire older workers (e.g., Home Depot, Borders, Wal-Mart, etc.). But do not limit your search to these well-known companies.

Develop an observational mindset; note the number of seniors working in your local establishments. In some retirement communities, the local supermarket will be full of retirees working flexible time and full time, filling positions others may not want.

If you want retail work (which will pay on an hourly basis), look around and see what interests you. Do you know people who work at these stores? Contact them first to ask about the work conditions before you go for an interview.

The key is to follow an interest if you have one. If, for example, you love to read, Borders or Barnes & Noble are the first places to look. Or, if you have some home improvement skills, try Home Depot, Lowe's, or the neighborhood hardware store. If your hobby is cooking, Williams-Sonoma or similar stores may be the ideal place for you to apply. The important objective is to find work that will satisfy you.

After you have narrowed down your list of stores, visit them to ask about the hiring procedures. Invariably, whether the store is hiring or not, you will be given an application to fill out.

If you are only interested in part-time employment, be sure to ask, "Does the company offer a flexible work schedule?" The term "flexible" is relative, so it is vital to learn how the company defines the phrase in terms of hours per day or days per week.

There is no need to contact corporate headquarters of the megastores or to do extensive research about the company online; the answers to your work questions will be given locally. Remember, these retail positions undergo a high turnover of personnel so you can be somewhat selective about the job you choose, as positions will always be available.

The Mall and Shops Within the Mall

A trip to the mall will offer countless other employment opportunities. Your first stop should be the mall's human resources office. Many of the larger megamalls are constantly looking for qualified people to work for the mall facility itself in positions such as product demonstrator.

Every individual shop within the mall can represent an employment possibility. The same procedure for inquiring about hiring applies at these mall shops as at the larger, national chain stores. Naturally, any department stores located inside the mall will have the greater number of possible openings and afford a wider choice of the retail experience.

A cautionary note: If you do not see people your age behind the counters of certain stores, it may be that the company prefers younger workers because of the image of the store or the physical demands of the job, such as lifting heavy objects, moving displays, etc. However, you can go ahead and apply if you wish; the worst outcome is that you fill out an application and never hear back.

Best Tips for Retail Work

A smart strategy to learn whether you enjoy retail or not, is to apply for a job before the holiday season. In a short period of time, usually from Thanksgiving to the middle of January (when the sales end), you can test the retail experience when store traffic is at its peak. Don't forget that most stores offer sizable employee discounts on merchandise even to the part-time employee. This can represent a significant savings for you depending on where you work, in addition to the income the position generates.

We have friends who fill in annually during the holiday season at the swank Fifth Avenue stores in New York City and who also take advantage of the discounts to buy quality clothing and accessories at significant savings. They love the work and delight when surprised acquaintances spot them behind the counter and ask, "What are you doing here?"

The two-month holiday work period should impart the real-world experience of retail. Some of the questions for self-assessment are:

✔ Was it too stressful?
✔ Was it remunerative for the time spent and taxes taken out?
✔ Were the hours flexible enough for you?
✔ Did you miss holiday events by working?
✔ Was it physically exhausting?
✔ Did you enjoy it?

Other Local Resources

Consider the work environment in your town or city or the neighboring area. In this space exist many other job opportunities. Before you knock at the door of every business, retail, or service center, narrow down the kind of job you want to ask about.

For example, local hospitals and medical centers need staff, and there are many openings within the medical service field that do not require any advanced training. These will be maintenance or service positions, usually, at a low-paid hourly rate.

A more relaxed medically oriented job is a receptionist in a doctor's office or a dentist's practice. Your own physicians or private dentist are possible job opportunities. Let the doctors know of your work search. Also ask if they can network you to colleagues who practice in the same building or medical center.

The ReWorked Life

Engineer to Restaurateur

Bob Wasky spent twenty-eight years working as a mechanical engineer with Baltimore Gas and Electric Company. When it came time to take early retirement at age fifty-three, he not only gave thought to where (Holden Beach, North Carolina) but also spent time considering what work activity he wanted to do now that he no longer had to work nine to five for the public utility.

His mind drifted back to 1971, when he was drafted into the army and was trained as a cook. He had enjoyed cooking, particularly baking, and he carried the hobby over after he left military service.

Wasky realized that the ability to plan and make meals for army personnel thirty-plus years ago would not translate to a career in the food-service business. He enrolled at a local cooking school and spent a year expanding his knowledge of food preparation.

When he completed the cooking course, he started to look for small local restaurants for sale. A few months later, he purchased Archibald's in Holden Beach. He changed the menu to high-quality seafood, fresh produce, and bakery items.

The area swells with tourists in the summer beach season when Wasky and his wife work ten hours or more a day. The restaurant has proved a modest financial success, but equally important, his Maryland crab cakes and homemade pastries are what draw customers in again and again.

Wasky was able to resurrect an old passion, and with some advanced training, take that love and translate it into a successful business. His retirement is filled with joy and the wonderful aromas that come from freshly baked goods.

Temporary Agencies

A quick way to see what's out there and what companies are paying for flexible-time workers is to contact one or more of the temporary agencies located in your town or city. Many will test your proficiency in word processing or spreadsheet skills before considering placing you in a position. At the outset, make sure to ask what positions they specialize in.

The temp agency takes a percentage from your wages, usually for as long as you work at the company where they placed you. Your salary check and the end-of-year W-2 form will come from the temp agency. If the company decides to hire you full time, it will negotiate a fee with the temp agency to "buy out" your contract, and you will become a bona fide employee of the company.

There are nationally known entities such as Kelly Services, which has been in this business for over sixty years. Many others are easily found in the Yellow Pages under "Employment Agencies" and under "Employment Contractors–Temporary Help."

A tip about temporary agencies: Not all of these agencies deal with office placements in the bookkeeping, receptionist, word processing, and administrative areas. Some deal with technical placements that require advanced or specialized training. But there are other agencies that may afford a new opportunity to the senior looking to do something different. These agencies seek butlers, nannies, drivers, housekeepers, caretakers, personal assistants, chefs, and so on.

Some of the larger temp agencies like Kelly have instituted a special program to place older adults. Soon, many more of these placement agencies will have programs like this as the demand for this valuable resource increases.

Executive Recruiters

For those who seek full-time employment, whether in the same career field or a new one, it is helpful to contact an executive recruiter. The best place to start is with recruiters with whom you have worked before. Because of their contacts, they may know of companies that are looking not only for full-time workers but also for project/consulting work, which might allow you more flexibility in your hours. If you are planning to move to another city or state for retirement, see if your recruiter has contacts in that area.

In the technical and scientific world, there is a developing brain drain of qualified individuals as boomers start to retire early. If there are no replacements for these retirees, companies will have to recruit older people with skills, often using executive recruiters to do so.

Working for Your Children

Depending on your situation this might be a possibility. We've included a "ReWorking Expert Advice" section that addresses the positive and negative aspects of this type of employment.

One option to consider if your children are working parents is offering to take care of the grandchildren during the day. This can be a way to generate income, spend time with your grandchildren, and help out family members. Though you might initially feel sensitive about charging for your services, don't be. This fee is vital if you need income, and your son or daughter would have to pay (often at exorbitant rates) another person for in-house day care.

The Senior Community Service Employment Program

The reality in the United States is that some seniors exist at bare subsistence levels. Many, as they age, cannot continue working a full week. The Senior Community Service Employment Program (SCSEP) offers applications to any low-income seniors seeking work and income assistance. Although its funding comes through the federal government, it is run through state and local community organizations.

The program is authorized through the U.S. Department of Labor Employment & Training Administration and provides part-time community-service employment for people fifty-five years of age and older who qualify due to low income levels. Family income must not exceed 25 percent of the U.S. government's stated poverty level. More guidelines can be found on the U.S. Health and Human Services Web site. Special consideration is given to veterans over sixty years old, or their spouses or widows. The jobs usually pay the state minimum wage and are run through state department of labor organizations.

These SCSEP jobs also provide on-the-job training and a chance to learn new skills. Many seniors can use them to become familiar with computers, for example, and perhaps leverage these abilities to higher-paying employment.

On average, people in this program work twenty hours per week. The work usually is directed to community-service activities, which include day-care centers, senior centers, schools, and hospitals.

To find out more about this program and how it operates in your state, telephone 877-US2JOBS (872-5627).

Jobs for Now and in the Future

Asked why he robbed banks, Willy Sutton said, "Because that's where the money is."

The U.S. Bureau of Labor Statistics predicts that the following occupations will add the most new positions between 2004 and 2014. It will be helpful to review these possibilities as you look to find new work or to consider changing your existing job.

✔ Retail sales
✔ Registered nurses
✔ Post-secondary teachers
✔ Customer sales and service representatives
✔ Janitors
✔ Waiters and waitresses
✔ Food preparers and servers
✔ Home health aides
✔ Nursing aides
✔ General and operations managers

Some of these jobs require advanced training, and you may not be able to do those jobs that are physically demanding.

Sales

This is a broad field that includes many job possibilities. Businesses are always looking for people to sell, and the classified sections are full of opportunities. Often, it is the quickest way for someone out of work to find employment.

Nevertheless, with a commission system built into the payment, it is not a quick guarantee of instant money. As well, the person who chooses sales as an option will have to undergo some training to learn the product or service.

ReWorking Expert Advice

Becoming an Adjunct Professor

Another place to look for part-time work is at a nearby college or university. The prospect of teaching provides a stimulating challenge to those people in search of interesting work, especially on a part-time basis. And being around young people will help keep you feeling young.

Some schools require an advanced degree such as a master of business administration (MBA). But qualified certified public accountants with only bachelor's degrees will also find positions. Often, colleges giving courses in areas such as retailing will be interested in good life experiences as background for teachers.

As a rule, institutions of higher education do not actively seek out nonprofessionals to fill in teaching positions for their curriculum; they have enough full-time professorial staff and graduate teaching assistants. But occasionally a college or university—particularly those that offer many graduate and undergraduate business courses and nighttime adult-education business classes—will use the services of adjunct professors possessing related work experience. The opportunities are greater at community colleges, which do not have graduate programs or many teaching assistants.

The two main benefits of adjunct professors to the universities and colleges are that they provide real-world experience, which interests students, and they are a great value for the money. A part-time adjunct will receive only a salary without FICA payments or pension payments—and a substantially lower salary than a tenured professor gets.

A university is faced with losing the revenue if a class is canceled, so they must find someone to teach it. The use of adjuncts has become a popular solution if teaching staff are busy with other courses.

We are two people who took this path to ReWorking their retirement. Bob Gorman is an Adjunct Professor of Marketing and Management at the University of North Carolina–Wilmington, and Allyn Freeman is the Adjunct Professor of Marketing at Adelphi University's ABLE program in New York City.

Many businesspeople will seek to do some kind of teaching when they retire, either informal volunteer work or on a more formal basis. Colleges or universities near home can provide this type of employment. Importantly, these adjunct professorships can last for many years and provide an anchor of stability.

The following hints and tips worked best for us. Freeman had the advantage of following Gorman's advice. Although we sought positions as businesspeople, those with proven talents in other areas (e.g., writing, painting, scientific and technical knowledge) can substitute their individual proficiency in place of the following business examples. An advanced degree in the specialty helps, but it is not mandatory.

Seasonal Hiring

Universities usually slot courses two to three months in advance. To this end, the optimum time to solicit for an adjunct professor's position is May to June for the fall semester, October to November for the winter term, and April to May if a summer session is offered. Last-minute withdrawals by teaching personnel may open up spots as the beginning of the semester approaches with larger-than-expected enrollment. The college wants to close such gaps quickly, especially when it has full student enrollment. A cancelled class means a loss of revenue.

The Directory of Colleges and Universities

Go to the local library and find the latest edition of *Barron's Profiles of American Colleges.* The listings are divided by states to facilitate locating those schools nearest you. Once you have found a college of potential interest, scan the list of people and jot down the name of the dean of the business school. (This may appear as "College of Business," "School of Arts and Sciences," or "School of Professional Studies.") In the absence of any business listing, write to the president of the college. Confirm all this information at the university's Web site.

Cover Letter and Resume

Draft a short letter that indicates your interest in an adjunct professor's job, a one-paragraph narrative on related experience (for example, "I have been a CPA for the past thirty-five years and am qualified in all areas of standard accounting practice"), and enclose a recent resume (in academic circles, called a curriculum vitae). Gorman had success searching out the e-mail addresses of the prime contacts at the universities and attaching a downloaded file, while Freeman employed the hard-copy letter.

Offer an Opportunity to Meet

Once you've made the initial contact with the appropriate person at the university or college, ask if it would beneficial to make an appointment to meet. The last statement can be modified with a specific date if your intention is to apply for a position at a school in a place where you intend to visit and stay for months. You can always follow up with a phone call for the home or away institutions.

Keep a folder of replies. Our experience is that more than 85 percent of the schools will reply to your solicitation with a negative answer. Many of these institutions have a full contingent of

available personnel and don't anticipate any teaching slots opening. But your folder will preserve the names of contacts. You will
want to update the list for reapplication next year.

List the Reasons Why You Want to Teach

If one or more of your solicitations generates a personal interview, you must prepare for it. Draw up a list of reasons why you
want to teach. Our five:

1. I want to give something back to the next generation.
2. I have real-world experience that should be shared.
3. I've always wanted to teach and am comfortable presenting in
    front of people.
4. The course work has been my life's interest.
5. Associates have always said I would make an excellent teacher.

Look up the school on the Internet, print out the course curriculum in the area of your expertise, and find the biography of
the person who will be interviewing you. This is especially important if it is a professor. Jot down any other information that you
find interesting about the school from its Web site.

Then we recommend that you write down five questions about
the course and the college. For example:

1. What's the student body like?
2. What is the textbook for the course?
3. Can you invite other people as guest lecturers?
4. Why is there an opening?
5. What is the expected enrollment in the course?

Always ask for the syllabus that was used in the past semester.
See if you can contact the person who taught the class the semester before. Sometimes certain courses are only taught by adjunct
professors. If you do receive a name, contact that person and ask
about the course, tests, term papers, and students.

The Interview

Dress well (jacket and tie for men, professional appearance for women) for this interview. Be as well dressed as, or better dressed than, the interviewer. Be sure to get directions for where on campus to go and, importantly, where to park. Arrive on time—but you knew that.

The interview is the last and most important step in the process of being hired. It is important to enter the interview room with a positive attitude; you want to exude interest and confidence.

Follow up with a thank-you by e-mail, and include some other credit or award you did not mention in the interview. From this moment on, there's nothing to do but wait. Three weeks before the start of the semester, if you haven't heard anything, send an inquiry about your status.

Even with great credentials, a super interview, and a strong interest in teaching, it is timing and opportunity that are the determining factors in obtaining an adjunct professorship. The variables to employment that you cannot control are returning faculty and student enrollments. If and when a teaching position arises, it will prove a rewarding experience.

* * *

A Final Note

One last piece of advice: If nothing materializes from one of the places in your job search list, do not discard it. Continue to check back on a timely basis.

7 Jobs Online

> *"Getting information off the Internet is like taking a drink from a fire hydrant."*
> —Mitch Kapor

Online job sites are proliferating at an exponential rate. Moreover, the boomers' coming of age is itself resulting in an upsurge of more Web sites offering advice and selling travel, insurance, assisted living, real estate, etc., to the increasing population of people over age fifty.

For those who do not have Internet access at home, every public library offers this capability if you cannot access the Internet at work or through family or friends. Often there are helpful people at the library who can assist the neophytes in navigating the technicalities of Google and Yahoo, and assist in performing other computer-related tasks.

Caution: If you are looking for a job online, you will experience an informational overload. For example, if you use Google and type in, "Jobs for seniors," millions of listings will come up. Type in "Senior organizations" and you will see many hundreds of millions of listings.

With a little guidance and direction, common sense, and trial and error, you can use this potentially valuable resource in your job search. However, bear in mind that you will most probably find that next job offline and not online. The old tried-and-true standbys of personal networking, local bulletin boards, legwork, telephone calls, personal interviews, and the like will be the primary activities that will produce your next job.

Before You Search Online

One bit of advice is to create a separate e-mail address for your online work search. This will separate job-related messages from your personal mail. In addition, if you register with data banks, job boards, and associations, you will be bombarded with these e-mails long after you have found employment.

If giving personal information online is a new experience, list only your e-mail contact; listing your address or phone number is also acceptable, depending on your comfort level. Never indicate a social security number or a PIN number for a credit card; requests for these are signs of fraudulent scammers or identity thieves looking for personal information. If, on the other hand, your association publishes a trade book with member names and addresses and requires a credit card as a method of payment, you should have every confidence of a safe and secure transaction. (A padlock symbol in the corner of the browser window indicates a secure transaction.)

Online Employment 101

There is much (maybe too much) to read online regarding looking for and finding employment. Searching online can take lots of time and be an unproductive substitute for actually finding work.

It is easy and comfortable to sit in your home or office and surf the Internet to fill up a day or part of the day with search activity. After a number of hours of registering with sites, posting resumes, and e-mailing, you might feel convinced that you've accomplished something. Although online job sites do not publish annual success rates, some research organizations estimate that only about 2 percent of all jobs are found online. This compares with the estimated 4 percent of all positions found from newspaper advertisements. Both methods compare badly with personal contacts, which have a 40 percent success rate. Be mindful of these percentages when you spend time online.

Once the novelty of looking for that next job online start to wane, you can go to better sites, even if it is only for updated information or new job postings. Here are some of the more prominent online search sites for the older worker.

AARP.org

The American Association of Retired Persons (AARP) is the single largest organization devoted to the social, medical, legislative, and commercial interests of persons fifty years and older. It is the nation's leading advocacy group for the older segment of the population.

AARP offers online advice, news stories of interest, access to medical plans, and other senior-related topics, including changes in social security and Medicare. Its current membership totals some 35 million, and this number is predicted to double to 70 million by 2015. As its numbers grow, the voice and power of this organization will also increase.

On the AARP site, there are short articles offering some basic advice on finding work, a retirement calculator, and a separate Money and Work section. The latter will take you to work-related chat rooms with other seniors and to the AARP's National Employer Team, a list of leading U.S. companies that hire older workers. Companies in this section include Home Depot, Borders, CVS Pharmacy, Kelly Services, and Quest Diagnostics.

AARP also offers discounts on insurance, travel, etc. that might be of interest. It is a large portal for information relating to its work advocating increased benefits for seniors.

It does not list jobs but it does list job search Web sites. In addition, its National Employer Team lists the best employers for people over age fifty and also provides online links to those employers.

Job-hunt.org

This is the one-stop shopping Web site for everything anyone at any age would want to know about how and where to look for employment. The information offered on this site is vast, so it will take a "big chew" to read and use all the data, links to other sites, downloaded articles, and so on. The first step is to scan the site and spot the reference or link that most interests you. Then, gradually, go step by step through the site.

Job-hunt.org offers two main advantages: first, it provides practical tips and easy-to-follow steps and guidelines to optimize online job searching; second, it offers an efficient and detailed linking service to many sites that are also of prime importance to the older job seeker.

For example, you are a click away from:

- ✔ State job listings for all fifty states
- ✔ State employment offices
- ✔ International jobs (separate category)
- ✔ Educational sites
- ✔ Governmental offerings
- ✔ Seasonal jobs
- ✔ Law enforcement, medicine, finance, and banking sites

Within the text pages of this site are numerous links to helpful online articles about job hunting (e.g., *Wall Street Journal*'s Career Journal.com), employment research data (e.g., America's Career InfoNet from the government), suggestions for books and magazines on job searching and careers, links to industry associations, and links to professional recruiters. The site also conducts interviews with career experts that are informative, instructive, and, importantly, free.

Additionally, Job-hunt.org provides valuable information on how to optimize the online job search, offering a savvy sixteen-critical-step guide. You can find tips on the Dos and Don'ts of e-mail techniques as well as much other useful information about searching for jobs online. However, keep in mind that although many jobs are advertised on the Internet and in newspapers, the probabilities are high that you will find that next good job through networking.

SeniorJobBank.org

SeniorJobBank.org is a not-for-profit site devoted solely to job listings offered to seniors state by state. It provides statistics on the over-fifty segment and other linking information to associations dealing with aging and retirement. It relies on companies and organizations to post jobs.

On days that we accessed the site, we did not find an abundance of offerings. For example, companies in North Carolina posted only two jobs, neither within driving distance of home base. When we typed in "New York," some of the jobs were upstate and not accessible.

The greater the number of people who use the site, the less chance that you will be the candidate selected. Maybe, over time, more employers may use this site for job postings. On a positive note, the site's statistical information always proved useful and informative.

RetirementJobs.com

This is an excellent online site for seniors. It was started by a group of human resource professionals who saw the growing need for people to find jobs in their later years. In addition, it uses the valuable input from the Center on Aging and Work/Workplace Flexibility at Boston College's Graduate School of Social Work. This is one of the premier institutions involved in analyzing ongoing problems and solutions for seniors in the workplace.

The employment service is free for job seekers. Prospective employers post open positions to the site, which then makes its database available to qualified job seekers.

Other Senior Sites

Here are additional senior work sites for you to peruse. These are similar to the Senior Job Bank in that they are also dependent on companies or organizations posting job openings on a daily basis.

✔ *www.2Young2Retire.com* Posts jobs daily
✔ *www.Seniors4Hire.org* A national career center for people fifty years and older
✔ *www.ExperienceWorks.org* Provides training for low-income, rural Americans

You should visit these sites and register (all are free), but do not get your expectations high that the magical job will pop up today or tomorrow. Remember to register under your new job-hunting e-mail address.

Advice When Looking Online

As you register at various employment sites, you should avoid any location that wants you to pay money up front for registration, resume assistance, or any other "deluxe" services charged at a premium.

The most egregious sites collect resumes and, after registration, immediately offer links to educational organizations or other paid-for career-related services. Though our profiles indicated master's degrees in business administration, undergraduate institutions linking through these paid sites popped up windows offering us coursework. With the wealth of free online postings and information available, there is no reason to pay money for information that is generic or isn't applicable to you.

Craigslist.org

This ubiquitous Web site provides job listings to more than 100 community sites in the United States. Once you have clicked your city, you will find jobs posted alphabetically by type. These are updated every day.

Many of the listed jobs are entry-level and intern positions. The people posting on Craigslist anticipate that respondents will be under thirty years of age, and that is why the words "intern" and "assistant" appear so frequently. However, these might be opportunities for you.

If you have a service that can be offered from a workstation at home, don't limit your search just to the city in which you live. Many creative services such as art illustration or writing will not require a personal contact or visit and can be pitched and obtained long distance.

Job Boards

A number of online job sites offer job seekers free registration. The sites' revenues come from employers posting job opportunities. In the past, some Fortune 500 corporations have experimented with posting jobs to these sites.

These sites are known in the employment vernacular as "job boards" and include *Monster.com, CareerBuilder.com,* and others. *Monster.com* is the most popular Internet employment site, rated the number-one online job site. It is free for prospective employees.

Producing Your Own Web Site

Creating a personalized career Web site is fast becoming a new technique for every person who wants to use this innovative method to convey more information than a posted resume in text form. Think of this as establishing your own brand, similar to a major corporation branding a product.

A Web site can include an expansive graphic presentation with color, pictures, and even sound. It can be as many pages as you like.

Consider the site a new business development tool where your past job background is the product being advertised. You can list references but request that interested parties contact you to receive these names and their addresses or telephone numbers. Another outstanding feature of personalized Web sites is that they are inexpensive and affordable. Yahoo and Google both offer frequent and ongoing discounts to sign with their services.

On Yahoo's Web site, look to the left-hand column and click "Web hosting," and on Google click "Business solutions" at the bottom of the page. Both of these sites offer clear explanations of their basic services and how much additional cost there is for add-ons (most or all of which you will probably not need for a career site).

Finally, for a few dollars more per month, you can direct e-mail from this site to your career online e-mail address. Consider using an inexpensive techie from a local college to assist you in this process.

ReWorking Expert Advice

An Internet Business

For many people in retirement, the Internet seems like an easy and fun way to make additional income, often by expanding a hobby or interest into a business. However, starting an Internet business should be done with the same caution as opening a retail store, especially by those seniors who have not had Internet mail order experience before.

Yet, taking a flyer by starting a business on the Internet can be done at a relatively inexpensive cost. It is also a great introduction to entrepreneurship, which is markedly different from most people's former company-based careers.

As detailed earlier, Ernie DelMonico is the owner of DelMonico Hatter, a New Haven, Connecticut–based cap and hat store. In 2002, the retired banking software entrepreneur decided to see if he could revitalize the moribund haberdashery business by mounting a site on the Internet.

After five years of Internet experience, DelMonico witnessed total gross company sales increase fivefold, the upsurge coming solely (and measurably) from newly found Internet sales. Over the five-year period, he and his staff became experts in the intricacies of advertising and positional placement on the popular and frequently used Google and Yahoo sites and on which software to use for assessing the search engine results.

DelMonico shares his empirical answers to the most frequently asked questions about starting up and doing business on the Internet.

Q. *What are the preliminary steps before making a decision to start a Web site?*

A. List the products you want to sell and then, one by one, type them into the Google and Yahoo search engines to ascertain how many other businesses also sell similar merchandise. If the Internet is inundated with similar products, the probabilities of success may be limited unless the new site owns a niche no one else has exploited, such as higher- or lower-priced goods, imported products, and so on.

Q. *What is the most important feature of a Web site?*

A. Internet customers who click the site's first, or home, page must immediately be assured that the Web site is an established business that offers the merchandise in the style and price range they seek. The Web site must have familiar and easy-to-follow directions to offer payment by credit cards, and a prominently advertised security safety feature.

Q. *Is payment by credit cards mandatory?*

A. Absolutely. Acquiring these credit card payment options is easy. But the new business owner must understand how the cards work, the percentage charged by the credit card company, and how long after payment the proceeds will be transferred from the credit card company into the business's bank account.

Q. *What happens initially when a business site is first posted?*

A. Don't expect any results for about two months. That will be the time it takes the powerful search engines to discover the site. A tip is to click daily on the one or two words that characterize the business (e.g., massage oils, fishing reels, organic peanut butter, etc.) to see if and when the site appears. Importantly, when it does show up, how far down the list does the site appear after other similar sites, and on what page?

Q. *How do Google and Yahoo build site traffic through payments?*

A. Basically, the e-retailer can pay the two mega search engines and listing companies via a wide range of fee opportunities to acquire a more prominent placement on their sites after a user has typed in a word or group of words. The options of how to advertise are explained on each site (Google on the bottom of the page and Yahoo on the lower left-hand side). The advantages are many, particularly if a site can achieve either a top position on the page or be listed among the initial ones on the first page. But the costs for obtaining these prime positions can be considerable, especially if there are multiple payments for many words.

There are two kinds of payments on Google, for example: a set monthly fee for placement on the top one or two positions on its page, and (with Yahoo also) a payment for each time a person clicks onto your site.

Q. *Can you explain the concept of "words" in greater detail?*

A. Assume the site sells homemade jams. To be listed prominently on Google or Yahoo, the Internet company wants the daily traffic to be directed to its site for many words the consumer might type in, such as "jams," "jellies," preserves," and "marmalade." The search engines will charge separate fees for each word. Further, imagine these products are "organic," then this word—probably in conjunction with one or two of the others—might also constitute an additional charge.

Q. *Can e-retailers customize the type and scope of the placements they buy on Google or Yahoo?*

A. Yes. If, for example, you operate a motel in Rockville Centre, Long Island, and know that most of the customers come from the

Metropolitan New York City area, you can restrict the word placement to the zip codes where the potential motel clients live. You can also buy days of the week or specific times of the day. These can all be ordered and modified online. Finally, a site can indicate its budget, and the search engines will modify and tailor an advertising buy based on the amount of money available for spending.

Q. *Do you consider the Google and Yahoo purchases a value for the money?*

A. Yes. First of all, via the Internet, DelMonico Hatter has virtual e-stores in Chicago, Providence, and both Portlands without any rental charge. That's the enormous benefit of e-retailing. It brings our products into millions of homes in the United States and overseas. In addition, we incur no salesperson's labor cost—the site describes the hats in detail and lists the price. We can eliminate a word or a product in a click if data indicate that it is not profitable for the store.

Q. *Do you have interesting observations or facts about Internet selling?*

A. One surprise for us was the greater sales of our imported, higher-priced hats. In New Haven, we have a limited number of customers interested in these more expensive models, but throughout the country we now can reach many thousands of men who want to own these deluxe models (e.g., Borsalino). One curious note was that about 10 percent of men are colorblind, so we had to adjust the color of our printing to allow these men to read the offers. Finally, the Internet also increased our New Haven in-store retail trade, with customers traveling as much as two hours to visit us after learning about us on the Web site.

Q. *Would you recommend seniors embark on an Internet business?*

A. I would recommend that anyone do a lot of homework before-hand. The costs to enter are quite low when compared to other kinds of brick and mortar businesses. But, again, how much business can a new company or online store do? The Internet seems easy but it is not.

* * *

A Final Note

In regard to job postings, the Internet's biggest drawback is that it serves as a potential advertiser for every job opportunity in the world, a huge employment smorgasbord where there are too many listings and too many people waiting in line.

Its greatest benefit lies in the delivery of useful addresses, telephone numbers, and Web sites for the more direct, up-front, and personal job pursuits. In this capacity it replaces a trip to the library and the tedious photocopying of lists of companies and organizations.

One of the prime reasons to go online for employment research is to find short-term or full-time retirement work in another location. By investigating online ahead of time you can form a realistic idea of what may be available in communities in which you are planning to relocate for your retirement.

Don't forget also that some companies now only advertise open positions on their own Web sites.

8 Resume, Cover Letter, and Interview

"Resume: a written exaggeration of only the good things a person has done in the past, as well as a wish list of the qualities a person would like to have."

—Bo Bennett

The resume, cover letter, and interview represent the nuts and bolts of the job-application process. The resume and cover letter are the tools you use to initiate contact. The interview is where you must shine. Our word of advice: Do not let these employment requisites cause you undue stress. Landing the job may be important but it shouldn't summon up the nerve-racking anxiety of career days past with overwritten resumes and intense my-life-depends-upon-it interviews. At this point in your life you are looking for job—not positioning yourself in a career. Remember this distinction, as it is important in how you present yourself and your credentials.

The Resume

Do a one-page resume, and that's it. Make it simple and informative. Since you are older—and the jobs offered are substantially lower in importance in your life than past career work—you will need to adapt the resume to the demands of the job marketplace.

We suggest emphasizing skill sets and experience:

1. **Eliminate dates.** Dates flag age. Dates say long ago. Dates might say "out of touch" to some hirers. In the absence of dates, the interviewer will have to look for aptitude and experience. Remove dates of college graduation or graduate degree dates. Do not write the number of years worked at a company or organization.

2. **Include only the past ten years' experience.** That should be sufficient to indicate the extent of your capabilities. Funnel the interest to this period and not to work in the distant past. The exception to this rule is if some experience further back has specific application to the current position. Say, for instance, that twenty-five years ago you worked in Puerto Rico and learned Spanish, which you have had no reason to use in any other job. Today, this dormant skill adds a plus to your resume and can open new doors in the job market.

3. **Do not reduce titles.** Be proud of what you achieved and how high up you rose in prior assignments. There is an unsubstantiated fear that a senior who attained a lofty title will seem overqualified for a position and therefore will not be considered a candidate for the job. We find this nonsense. If you are applying for a job to drive a school bus, the important factor is the ability to drive carefully and not whether—as the former Admiral of the Fleet—you might consider the task below your station.

4. **Cite accomplishments accompanied by brief examples.** Enumerate achievements in your past employment with a list of success-oriented verbs such as "expanded," "managed," "increased," and "developed." Next to each verb, write a sentence listing the specifics of that accomplishment. These will become the talking points during the interview.

5. **List awards or honors.** Sing your own praises about past successes that occurred in and out of work. You goal is to have the resume stand out among the clutter of the other applicants. If you can refer to some honor or award, put it on the bottom of the page.

Additional points: The resume must list at the top of the page your contact information. Do not write "References furnished upon request." Importantly, give the resume to someone else to spell check and to look for typos.

Finally, many resumes will begin with an Objective at the top, which can be altered for each specific job applied for. This aspect of the resume is more important for retirees, as employers will tend to question why someone who was a manager or executive is applying for the position. State your intention in the objective section: "A retired insurance executive looking for a part-time claims adjustment position."

The ReWorked Life

School Administrator to Boatman

Tom Hetherington worked as an administrator in a Maryland school district for twenty-five years. The town where he worked was not far from Chesapeake Bay, and he took a keen interest in boating, eventually owing a twenty-six-foot craft.

He wanted to spend more time pursuing the boating hobby after retirement with some thought to also finding work in the boating industry. When he and his wife searched for a retirement home, it was important to them to find a community on or near the shore. Finally, when retirement came, he built a home near Southport, North Carolina, a stone's throw from Onslow Bay and, farther out, the Atlantic Ocean.

After settling in, he applied for and was hired to do retail sales in a local marina where he worked for two years. But working at a marina did not provide the same good feeling as being out on the sea.

Finally, management transferred him from the boating section to work at a newly opened convenience store in the marina. He was farther away from boats and boating than before. With enough income from social security and pensions, he did not need the $9.25 an hour wage, and he quit.

When he assessed the job at the marina, he realized that if he wanted to work part-time in the boating business, he had to improve his seafaring knowledge and boating skills to become a bona fide professional. He enrolled and passed a captain's course and is looking to begin a chartered boat business, which will take him out to sea.

Resume Writing Assistance

A sizable cottage industry has sprouted up offering advice (for a price) on the best way to compose a resume. This can be valuable, mainly to those people just starting out in a career, or changing an important one in midlife.

Online, you can find numerous Web sites that offer free examples of resumes. Some will require registration. If you haven't written a resume in a long time, go to any of the free sites and print out a few resumes as examples.

Amazon.com, the online seller of books and other items, lists more than 1,000 titles under the keyword "resume." Bear in mind that every person who buys these books or consults with a professional writer or personal coach will turn out resumes that all resemble many others.

We say, forget these books. Forget contacting some resume writer to compose one for you. Do not use expensive twenty-eight-pound heavy paper stock with writing done in fancy fonts. The probability is that the money invested in this will not result in a greater success rate.

The Cover Letter

A job application needs a cover letter to accompany a resume. We prefer a first paragraph that states simply, "I am writing in response to your job opening (or ad) for a part-time hardware sales representative."

If you possess a specific background that can indicate past experience, the next paragraph should refer to this former work. For instance, continuing the example, "For five years, I worked in a similar retail sales position at Hegeman's Hardware Store in Pawtucket, Rhode Island."

If the letter is an open inquiry about general employment, write instead "I am writing to inquire about possible job openings." Or, if you can pinpoint a specific occupational interest within the company or organization, then mention it as follows: ". . . to inquire about possible bookkeeping openings." If you write the latter, be sure to reveal what prior experience you had in this field.

Be sure to mention that the resume is included. The last paragraph states that you will follow up this letter with a telephone call in the next two weeks.

That's all you need: a cover letter that is short, informative, direct, and, of course, with zero grammatical and spelling mistakes.

The Myth of the Younger Interviewer

Every recent article about interviews of older workers begins with the fact that the person doing the interview will be younger than you are. So what? These tedious references to the age difference are giving younger people a bad rap and imply that they will not know how to talk to a senior.

While you are going to encounter negative interviewers in any job search at any age, we think the presumption that a senior should automatically anticipate such an experience is nonsense. The person in the interview is a trained professional who has interviewed hundreds if not thousands of people, many of them over fifty years old.

The fact is that you are the age you are; dwelling on the age difference will only make you feel uneasy about the process. If you accept the premise that the younger interviewer is going to be put off by your age, it will trigger a negative reaction that will act as a big minus for your job prospects.

Moreover, in today's litigious climate, no company or organization wants to be accused of age bias or discrimination. The interviewer's goal is to fill positions within the organization, not turn off potential applicants.

We're not saying that instances of bias or inappropriate questions won't occasionally occur. Simply deflect them or gracefully conclude the interview (depending on whether or not they are egregiously offensive) and re-evaluate whether this is the best place for you after all.

In our interviews with seniors and retirees looking for work, we found no one who narrated a case where the interviewer asked, "Can you keep up?" What we did find was that interviewers of all ages welcomed seniors and asked questions about skills and experience. It should be no different for you.

The Interview

The interview process is important for seniors but it does not require lengthy hours of preparation and study. Do some basic preparation work, show up on time, and relax during the interview. The interview is a two-way conversation with questions and answers on both sides of the table.

The best way to prepare for the main question, "Tell me a little about yourself," is to have a well-rehearsed and dynamic thirty-second commercial about your accomplishments. Practice this talk in front of friends and, if you can, use a video camera to see if you come across as confident and conversational.

Here are our basic suggestions for making the interview better:

Do some homework: Find out beforehand a few details about the company or organization. It is a welcome courtesy. The main point to research is of course, what the company does.

Practice your presentation: Ask a friend or spouse to be the interviewer and rehearse the process. Answer these three questions: "Why do you want to come work here? What qualifications do you have to do the job? Do you have any questions for me?" When finished, ask for an appraisal.

Relax and be positive: The key to getting the position is to sound upbeat about the prospect of doing this job for the organization. Interviewers want you to succeed; they want to fill the job.

Emphasize maturity: This represents one of the main attributes that set you apart from younger applicants. Give examples to embellish seasoned interpersonal skills in life and in work.

Be up to date: The interviewer will want to explore your knowledge of and experience with computers and other technology. Don't claim knowledge you don't have, but try to be up-to-date on the technological skills required by the job you're applying for.

Don't overstate your experience: Even if you were CEO, that's not the position for which you are being interviewed. If you refer to previous high-level career positions too frequently, the interviewer is apt to wonder if you'll try to exceed the boundaries of the advertised position.

Ask questions: Prepare two or three questions about the job that go beyond the salary and hours.

Bring references with you: Have two written references at hand in case the interviewer mentions that these will be needed. It saves time, and it shows you were cognizant of this possibility.

Ask about the timing of the decision: Be proactive and inquire when the interviewer will make a hiring decision.

The ReWorked Life

Teacher to Home-Care Companion

Gia Campos was born and educated in Manila. She graduated with a bachelor of arts degree from a Philippine university, immigrated to the United States, and began teaching Spanish at a Catholic high school. She was able to teach at this level because parochial schools did not demand the certification required by public schools.

Campos taught for thirty-one years and was laid off when the local diocese began consolidating and closing many of the grammar schools and high schools in the area where she lived. It was a shocking and unwelcome surprise, but gradual declining enrollment and outdated facilities had dictated the downsizing as a necessary economic move.

At age fifty-two, Campos was out of a job. She had no prospects to continue teaching at other Catholic high schools, and she could not transfer her years of teaching experience to public schools. She regretted never having obtained a master's degree in education and state certification. Her small pension did not cover living expenses.

Through her local church bulletin board, Campos offered her services as a companion to a few older parishioners. She possessed excellent housekeeping and cooking skills, and her English was fluent. She was thoroughly familiar with medical insurance forms. Importantly, she could also drive her clients to doctors' and dentists' offices for appointments.

As more elderly people from the church required her services, she started a referral organization to recruit other men and women in the local Philippine community. Currently, her income is greater than she ever made as a teacher, and she plans to expand her caregiving business.

ReWorking Expert Advice

Interview Approaches

This will cover both the job seeker's approach to the interview and the interviewer's point of view. It is important for job candidates to understand the questioner's goals and to provide answers that meet the specific expectations of the hiring criteria.

The interview process will often be the procedure that will decide whether you are hired. Repeatedly, we heard stories of friends and acquaintances who were keen on taking a new job only not to be selected after the interview. Often they remained unaware of the reasons why they did not move past this screening process, not comprehending that they failed to respond positively to the questions. Being passed over can create residual anger and disappointment that sometimes results in stopping the job search because of the bleak prospect of future rejection.

When we listened in detail to the interview questions posed and to the applicants' responses, we realized that there were two areas that needed clarification: the point of view of the person conducting the meeting and, more importantly, the attitude of the senior during the course of the interview.

For more expert guidance on this critical topic, we turned to Joie Smith, an outplacement, career, and executive search professional (*jsmith@touchstonepartners.com*). For more than twenty-five years, she has counseled terminated blue-collar and white-collar workers. For the past six years, she has been a managing director of TouchStone Partners VIP Search that deals with senior-level executive searches. To that end, she is knowledgeable about both sides of the interviewing process.

We departed from the question-and-answer format and instead divided this section into two parts, one from the perspective of the interviewer and the other containing smart tips for the applicant on handling the interview.

What the Interviewers Want

1. **They are looking for the intrinsic and unique experience of the older applicant.**

   Seniors are people who will add value to the company or organization because they have achieved many objectives over a lifetime of work. They have been successful in many non-work areas: buying and owning homes; starting and taking care of families; acquiring assets, including stock and bonds portfolios; and other civic, religious, and group accomplishments. It is the interviewer's task to discover this information because seniors have demonstrated responsibility and service that many younger applicants have not.

2. **They want to translate your past experience to the new job.**

   Today's interviewers are often aware that older workers have excellent work ethics. The generation born in the decade of the 1940s is respected for its willingness to work long hours, its goal orientation, and its capacity to take instruction. Importantly, the company can always teach new technical skills if you are not as proficient as younger employees in the organization. What cannot be taught is the work ethic that you possess.

3. **They want to conduct a meaningful interview.**

   The interviewers will probably attempt to draw out those accomplishments of which you are most proud. In many instances, this may be their initial question, allowing you to relax and to discuss non-employment activities. Further, they will probably want to discover where you have applied your talents. The questioner might also inquire about dreams and goals for the future. These informal questions do not mean that the interviewers are uninterested in successes from former careers, but they might ask about those after having established a comfortable rapport.

4. **They want to determine your compatibility with the company.**

They will try to sense if you can fit into this company's system and its corporate or organizational culture. Key to this probing will be an assessment of character: Are you someone who will be an asset to the company? You can answer by citing your accomplishments and repeat successes as well as volunteer efforts or problem solving in any area. Once interviewers are confident that you will be the value-added person they seek, they may ask about the specifics of your past career. But the likelihood is that the company is not looking to match specific past experience (e.g., accounting, sales, etc.) with the current job opening; it is looking for mature experience that it can tailor to the new job.

5. **They are seeking maturity.**

Your greatest asset is maturity, and most interviewers want to see evidence of this during the process. You have learned to receive instructions and to give them. Most important is that all those years of past experience translate to making better judgments that are vital in the workplace.

Advice for the Interviewee

For the interview you should dress neatly, arrive on time, and carry a resume in case it is requested.

1. **Communicate a positive attitude.**

You should exude a positive attitude during the interview. Have an affirmative, "Yes, I can do that job" mentality. Interviews at any age are always stressful, so it is important to try and reach a calm state before entering the room. You want to be able to convey an interest in the position and in the organization or company. The key is to exhibit an optimistic outlook about your possible performance in that job. Never be arrogant or convey a superior demeanor, no matter what the job is.

2. **Indicate flexibility.**

   Show a willingness to adapt. This may take the form of accepting irregular scheduling, including number of hours or days and a call for weekend work. Or it may mean agreeing to a request for additional training or coursework. Be alert to a sudden change in the nature of the job, arising from an unforeseen event at the company or organization. Someone may quit or be terminated, or a candidate may decide not to accept a job. This will leave the company with a job it has to fill in a hurry.

3. **Regard the future with enthusiasm.**

   The past was yesterday, and the job you want is today. Emphasize in the interview that the new job will bring with it new challenges and meeting new people. Do not dwell on the past, and don't subject employers to a long-winded account of former employment, how you rose to your title, and the way your previous employer did business.

4. **Convey a realistic self-appraisal.**

   You should be levelheaded about what you can and will do, so it doesn't make sense to try to be hired for a job for which you are unqualified. Further, you should have a clear idea of the number of hours and days you want to work and the physical requirements of certain jobs. Learn as much as you can about the job and the company before the interview.

5. **Be confident about the past.**

   This is just the next step toward a successful future.

Questions and Requests

One of the biggest problems for seniors in job interviews is asserting an "I'll work here on my terms only" attitude. Here are a few questions seniors ask that set off red flags for interviewers.

✔ "How long before I qualify for the next raise?"
✔ "How do I present my many ideas to the company?"
✔ "How much time off do I receive?"

It is okay to indicate specific needs that arise from health or energy levels. Here are a few examples of requests that are acceptable:

- ✔ "I need every Friday morning off from eight a.m. to ten a.m. for physical therapy."
- ✔ "I have to leave the office no later than five p.m. when my grandchild, who lives with me, comes home from school."
- ✔ "I need an ergonomic chair because of my back."

The ReWorked Life

Family Business to Teacher

Don Freedman ran his family's die-cutting operation, Freedman Cut-Outs, which had been founded in 1918 by his grandfather, also the inventor of 3-D glasses. At age fifty-three, Freedman was burned out by thirty-two years of the business's constant and stressful sales and service. He decided to sell the assets of the company, renovate the property that he owned, and generate supplemental income by renting space in the New York City building.

Freedman had two life goals: to perform in retirement some useful activity that he enjoyed, and to do it in or near a setting for his triathlon and skiing hobbies. He had purchased a home in the Berkshire Mountains of western Massachusetts, and it was here that he looked for the ideal ReWorking of his second career.

Freedman decided he wanted to teach high school and coach sports. The lack of any formal education courses ruled out employment in the public school sector. He volunteered to tutor students in math to get a foot in the door at a nearby private school, which did not require teaching certification. After he had tutored for two years, the school hired him full time as a math teacher.

To improve his professional teaching skills, Freedman enrolled at a nearby college and earned a second bachelor's degree in mathematics.

He began coaching judo, soccer, lacrosse, snowboarding, skiing, and rugby for both men and women. He also served as a rugby referee on the weekend.

His retirement is full-time work and relaxation.

The Next Interview

If you pass muster on the first interview, there may be a second interview. You should prepare for this one differently. The good news, though, is that you can consider yourself a bona fide candidate for the job. There are two possible reasons for a second interview:

1. **The supervisor wants to meet you:** The first interviewer has vetted your application and passed it on to the person for whom you might be working. This interview is different in many aspects from the first one because the supervisor will be looking to see if you can be part of her team. Examine the job description and list five specific attributes you possess that will help you contribute value to the job. Practice this part of the interview beforehand.
2. **A different job has surfaced:** The initial job discussed has been filled, but a new job exists and the company wants to investigate your potential interest. If you show enthusiasm about this new position, it may be offered to you.

* * *

A Final Note

The interview is the last and most important step in the process of being hired. It is important to enter the interview room with a positive attitude; exude interest and confidence. This is true at a company or at a college—sell yourself and your skill set.

9 Taking the Job and Going to Work

"If you do not want to work you have to work to earn enough money so that you won't have to work."

—Ogden Nash

Accepting a new post-retirement job will represent a new challenge and a break—physically, emotionally, and mentally—from your former career. It is important to prepare for this new challenge because you will have to rewire expectations, ambitions, and, most important, your own standards of performance.

The new job requires some behavior modification because it will not be a continuation of the old career with its familiar pluses and minuses. It is important to also realize that there will be a necessary readjustment to accommodate lowered expectations, since you may not receive the same kind of gratification—money, status, power—as you did from the prior career position.

You want to do well and are eager to begin, but if, over time, it doesn't pan out as anticipated and you quit, it is not as though your financial world will crumble. Consider the new job as an experiment in personal choice and freedom. This new work represents a chance perhaps to do something you enjoy or something you have been dreaming about for a long time.

Although the new job will provide many rewards, you do not have to make the same strong emotional commitment to it as you did with your former career. The new work should be less stressful and more enjoyable, and fill a personal need—financial, psychological, or both.

The ReWorked Life

Intelligence Expert to Deli Worker

Rita Montequin worked for the National Security Agency as an Information Systems Analyst. Her husband also worked at NSA, and for a time after he retired she continued to work full time. But with the disconnect in their daily schedules, and given that their grown children were settled elsewhere, Rita decided to take deferred retirement to allow the couple to move to a house on the North Carolina shore.

Initially, Rita described the change as "one big vacation"; then she began to experience post-retirement trauma. She did some short-term consulting in her old career and later turned to volunteer work, but neither provided the social interaction or the camaraderie of her past work in Washington.

While shopping at supermarket, she spotted a "Hiring Now" sign and was hired immediately to work in the deli department. It provided her with social interaction, some extra but not vital money, and a great deal of enjoyment, because for the first time in her working life, she was under no pressure.

The deli honeymoon lasted a year, but putting in all those hours on her feet started to take its physical toll. The supermarket did not want to lose such a good hire and switched her to cashier (twenty-six hours per week), then, realizing she had excellent management skills, made her a trainer of new cashiers.

She now assists the store's floral department in unpacking and setting out flower displays. She does this for free as a hobby at the supermarket after her daily cashier work. Her retirement days are filled with the sweet smell of flowers.

Preparation

Before you begin your new position, make a list of the job specifications and the most important duties that need to be performed. If you are unsure of what these are, clarify them with either the person who hired you or your new supervisor. After making a list of the duties, indicate the task that is the most important. Performing this assignment is key to success on the job. This simple exercise will help you concentrate and prioritize the duties.

Take the following example:

Tour Guide

Job Description: Guide for city walking tour, Monday through Friday, from 10 A.M. to 3 P.M. (last tour of day)

✔ Take people on informative, one-hour walking tour of city
✔ Have knowledge of environs, including past and current history
✔ Answer questions related to the sights seen on the tour
✔ Answer tourist-related questions (e.g., hotels, museums, shopping, etc.)

This exercise will clarify what you have to do and what you have to learn or be trained for in order to accomplish your tasks.

The First Day at Work

The job will seem strange and new and maybe less demanding than you anticipated. This is to be expected on your first day, and this feeling may persist into the first week. Time will change you from novice to an experienced worker.

It may be helpful to seek out other seniors at the workplace and find out some of the good things about this job. You can be more open with these questions with a fellow worker than with a supervisor.

At the end of each week for the first month on the job, fill out the following report card. On a scale of one to ten, with ten being the highest, rate how satisfied you were with these aspects of the job.

Job Satisfaction Calendar

	Week 1	*Week 2*	*Week 3*	*Week 4*
Work conditions				
Ability to do the job				
Coworkers				
Pay for the work				
Stress level				
Fun				
Satisfaction				
What you expected				
Commute				
Expenses				

After four weeks have passed on the job, compare the results. Has there been a positive progression with all the levels of satisfaction?

If, after a month, the scores in most of these categories are not above an average level, our advice is to go find another job that seems as if it will provide higher satisfaction. Why waste your time doing a job that brings in no reward or satisfaction?

The ReWorked Life

Lawyer to Witness Coach

Ed Wepprect combined an engineering undergraduate education with the post-graduate study of law and took this combined learning into a legal position at Lucent Technologies, a communications corporation. The company employed him for more than twenty years, mainly in its work with the federal government.

Over the years, Wepprect understood that Lucent's continually changing technology was fast outpacing his learning. When he turned fifty-five years old, he began to consider what else in life he could do. He was determined to find a second career in a field that interested him more.

Over time, he evaluated his strengths and weaknesses and realized that he wanted to continue in law but not do law. And he wanted to do this on a part-time basis as an independent contractor. When he researched further, he discovered that there existed one unusual field where he could use his legal knowledge of the federal government; he would prepare witnesses who were scheduled to appear in trials or depositions before the government.

The next step was to find law firms that offered this special kind of service. He composed an informed cover letter that sparked interest with a Texas firm that hired him. The firm contracts for the witness preparation jobs and passes on the details to Wepprect, who makes his own travel arrangements.

Wepprect enjoys the freedom, the work, and the modified job schedule. He has developed a deserved reputation as a lawyer with excellent witness preparation shills. He works when and how long he wants and enjoys a high measure of satisfaction.

Unrealized Salary Expectations

The job you accepted should be one that pays enough money to cover the difference between your total expenses and your combined sources of income. But assume that the new job does not bring in the wages you need to at least break even. It is better to generate some income than none. However, sooner or later you will have to tap into savings to make up the balance, or else find cost-cutting ways to lower monthly expenses.

If you have been forced to take work that will not make up the deficit, you have two main options to eliminate the shortage: For instance, a Saturday or Sunday job at a retail outlet, especially a job that pays commission, could bring in the needed money and also offer discounted clothing or other benefits.

First, find out when you can expect a pay raise and how much it will be. Then slot in the waiting time for you to qualify for this advance. If it is only a short time, and you can handle the monthly shortfall, stay on the job if you like it.

Second, try to find another job that can meet the minimum money that you need monthly. Unfortunately, you will only be able to look during free time. Our suggestion is to ask for weekend duty. Out of a five-day workweek, this will leave you two weekdays to concentrate on finding new employment and leaving you free for appointments and interviews.

If you continue to fall short each month, your enthusiasm for the job will diminish and your desire to perform it will decline.

The ReWorked Life

Plastics to Science Teacher

When David Moore retired from a long career in the plastics industry, he realized he had to find some involving way to pass the time. He had acquired a lifelong interest in science and wondered whether he could teach it at the college level as an adjunct professor.

Moore found an assistant professorship in physics at Reinhardt College in Georgia, where he began teaching astronomy and physics to liberal arts students. To increase the scientific knowledge needed to improve his teaching, he started taking National Science Foundation (NSF) Chautauqua Short Courses for undergraduate college teachers. These are free forums where leading scientific scholars conduct intensive three-day seminars at universities in the United States.

Being involved again in the study of science spurred Moore on to learn more about the college classwork he taught at Reinhardt. He took additional courses in astronomy at the National Radio Astronomy Observatory at Green Bank, West Virginia.

As his knowledge increased, so did the proficiency of his teaching. He appreciated that the more he learned, the greater the student interest in his classes became. He embarked on a course in meteorites at the Meteor Center near Flagstaff, Arizona, and recently finished an Excellence in Teaching astronomy course on the Big Island, Hawaii.

For Moore, the reawakening of an early appreciation in science provided a stimulating opportunity to rework retirement and to contribute to the badly needed next generation of physicists and astronomers.

Comments from the Field

We did an informal survey among many of the people interviewed for this book, asking them to describe some of the good aspects and some of the not-so-good aspects of returning to work in a different occupation. The responses were similar for both paid work and volunteer assignments.

THE GOOD THINGS

✔ Starting anew
✔ Generating additional income

✔ Meeting new people
✔ Having new challenges and opportunities
✔ Reducing stress
✔ Setting different goals and objectives
✔ Learning new skills
✔ Having a flexible work schedule

THE NOT-SO-GOOD THINGS

✔ Earning less income than in previous job
✔ Working in unfamiliar surroundings
✔ Having uncertain goals
✔ Losing status
✔ Being a worker, not a supervisor
✔ Enduring job drudgery
✔ Re-experiencing work-related stress
✔ Working below skill levels

The ReWorked Life

Marketing to Mold Removal

Ron Clifford enjoyed a long and productive career with Eli Lilly, working in its marketing department in many states and even for a while in Toronto and London. He was happy taking early retirement and looked forward to busy days of golf and tennis and doing lots of volunteer work at his church.

A previous hotel time-share experience convinced him that Hilton Head, South Carolina, was an ideal retirement location. His son and daughter also came there to live with their spouses and children.

His son-in-law started a new local business of home inspection and mold removal, which proved highly successful. Then the son-in-law's army reserve unit was called up for military service in Afghanistan. The family decided it was important for the home business to continue, looking ahead to the day when the son-in-law would return.

Clifford had to give up his full retirement to assume the daily operation of the new business. He was the only person with the time and the business skills to manage it. The new company proved a stimulating challenge, and he worked as many hours as when he was employed by Eli Lilly. His days were constantly busy and fruitful; he enjoyed meeting new people in the course of business. Under his stewardship, the firm grew substantially.

His son-in-law returned safely from his military service, and convinced Clifford to stay on assisting with the home inspection business. Clifford's unselfishness had saved an ongoing enterprise and the young family's livelihood, as well as giving him an unexpected but satisfying new career in retirement.

* * *

A Final Note

To summarize, after you have been in your new position for a couple of months you need to ask yourself: Is this job absolutely essential to me? Is it creating more stress than it is worth? Is it damaging my health? Am I getting true enjoyment from doing it?

If some form of the income is necessary, you may have to bite the bullet and stay in the job until you have another position. Continue your own searches that proved successful in finding this job, and another will appear on the horizon. But if the income is not essential and it starts to have all the negatives of a bad job, it is time to say goodbye.

10 Entrepreneur

*"The critical ingredient is getting off
your butt and doing something."*

—Nolan Bushnell

Perhaps the idea of starting your own business has been one of your lifelong dreams. Now with retirement looming on the horizon, you are strongly considering turning that vision into an entrepreneurial reality. Is it time to chase the dream?

Reasons for becoming an entrepreneur in your post-retirement years are the same as for doing it at any other time: being one's own boss, working a flexible schedule, and believing "the sky's the limit" to making money.

Entrepreneurial opportunities can be invigorating and exciting ways for you to keep busy and stay financially independent. If you spent your career in a corporate environment you are finally free, possibly for the first time in your life, from the restraints of a nine-to-five job, working in the confines of a closely controlled organization.

Entrepreneurial ventures can be as minimal a time and financial investment as selling a few items on e-Bay or as involved as operating a major franchise of a well-known, nationally advertised company. We found that some people over age fifty nurtured dreams of opening a bed-and-breakfast or beginning new careers in real estate sales. You will find "Expert Tips" in this chapter on both of these popular entrepreneurial possibilities.

However, you need to be cautious about entering into entrepreneurship for two primary reasons: the enterprise may not generate sufficient income to cover life's expenses, and a self-started business can expand exponentially and require large amounts of time and money that can drain your physical energy and savings.

The How and What of Going into Business

How many friends have mentioned to you, when they were ready to retire, that their dream was to open that charming motel? In New England? In the Carolinas? In New Mexico? Did any of them do this? Did any succeed?

A self-starting business is an excellent idea if done wisely with a realistic assessment of risk. Going into your own business full time needs study, long-term preparation, and, on occasion, professional advice from attorneys, accountants, or other people already in this business.

For more serious ventures you should generate business plans, do cost and risk analyses, and look at other economic variables if you have not worked in the field before. Yes, it's time-consuming, but these preparations are necessary for you to assess the costs and probabilities of success.

The downside is that if the venture fails, you may lose time and money. Herein lies a problem with the naive "sixty is the new forty" way of thinking: If an entrepreneurial project fails, you will not have the luxury of time to recoup the monetary loss.

Do You Have the Makings of an Entrepreneur?

Two questions to ask before you begin: First, do you have the personality to become your own boss? Second, why now? If you have been dreaming of starting your own business your whole life but avoided taking the plunge, why has arriving at this age suddenly convinced you to take the risk?

Not everyone can manage the entrepreneurial process, especially those who have been satisfied to work for years within a restricted organizational format with defined goals and narrow responsibilities. If you have prospered in an orderly business environment without individual risk-taking, going into business for yourself can turn out to be an emotional and financial minefield.

The traits and characteristics that make up a good entrepreneur are the same qualities that make a good inventor. You must be creative, forward-thinking, a decision-maker, and importantly, have the ability to self-start a project and turn it into a successful reality with determination and persistence.

Do you have these traits? Will you be willing to sacrifice a secure paycheck and a defined work schedule for the risks and rewards of doing something by and for yourself? The critical question: Is this how you visualized retirement?

ReWorking Expert Advice

Owning a Motel or a Bed-and-Breakfast

One of the dreams of some people when they retire is to open a bed-and-breakfast or a small motel and become involved in the hospitality business. They perceive this as a chance to spend pleasant times in an appealing area, meeting people from other parts of the country and overseas, and affording the opportunity to generate extra or needed income.

There are two other reasons why the concept is attractive: It offers a married couple a permanent place to live and work in retirement, and it seems like an ideal business for a husband and wife to do together, sometimes with the family.

Choices abound within the possible hospitality offerings, from a three- or four-room bed-and-breakfast to a hundred-room hotel. A small house can be converted into a B&B, zoning permitting, or you can buy an existing one. Prices will vary according to the size and age of the property and the popularity of the area.

You can also purchase motels of twenty or thirty rooms or less, or you can buy a property with multiple-room cottages. Many hospitality properties can be owned and operated in franchise agreements with well-known chains.

The work remains the same for a small or a large establishment. It is all about providing temporary housing, and on occasion food, to people who are traveling or on vacation.

The rise in the number of boomers reaching fifty will increase the number of semiretired or fully retired people who will take more leisure time and longer vacations. The bottom line is that the hospitality business will probably grow exponentially over the next ten to twenty years, especially in Sun Belt states, to accommodate the greater number of American seniors taking to the road.

To provide a realistic look at the opportunities and the pitfalls of entering into the hospitality business, we asked sisters Diane Brannen and Fran Panasci to provide advice, both supportive and cautionary, to someone considering entering the business. The two began working at their family's twenty-four-room Buffalo Hotel, which opened in Wildwood, New Jersey, in 1952. Later, they worked at a thirty-six-room motel called the Ocean Crest Lodge. Eventually, Fran opened her own motel, the Easterner in Southampton, Long Island, in 1979. Diane continued running motels in Wildwood until she sold off all her properties in 2003.

Work in the Business Before Considering a Purchase

We suggest that people find work in a small motel and learn firsthand about the business. Work in season when the traffic is highest and the greatest number of people arrive. Would-be buyers should learn every part of the operation, particularly the housekeeping and maintenance chores. These are the daily tasks owners must do if the staff does not show or the laundry delivery does not arrive. Housecleaning is laborious and constant and has to be attended to every day. The smaller the operation—such as a B&B or a motel with fewer than twenty beds—the larger the probability that the owners will have to do these daily tasks. It is more difficult to learn the operation of a big motel, and the degree of management skills increases because of the larger number of employees who have to be supervised.

Research the Area and the History of the Motel

Is the area growing or in decline? Try to ask other motel or B&B owners in the vicinity about business prospects. If possible, check with the town or county officials about new roads that might bypass locations you're considering, or plans for extensive municipal construction that could have an adverse affect on vehicular traffic. Who owns the properties on either side of the places that interest you? Do they have specific plans for other businesses? Ask real estate agents for the recent history of motel and B&B purchases to ascertain whether there has been a lot of buying and selling activity. This may not be a good sign—a warning of high turnover because of insufficient business. Do the owners belong to the local Chamber of Commerce? This is often a good indication of their involvement in and care for the community.

Seasonal or Yearly Business?

How seasonal is the B&B or the motel? Learning this fact will indicate whether an owner/manager will be occupied twelve months or only some months during the year. If it is a year-round rental, when does that leave time for your vacation? If seasonal, then most revenue for the year must be generated during the optimum months. If a spate of bad weather occurs during the primary season, expect income to drop dramatically. The shortfall will leave owners with a net loss for the season and no way to recoup money in the off-season.

The Size Determines Your Obligations

There is a lot of down time in a small place if the owner has hired staff to do the cleaning and the laundry service. At a vacation destination area, most guests will book ahead of time by e-mail, fax, or telephone so there is no need for someone to stay in the office all day. The important point is that on many occasions the owners will have time on their hands.

There Are Two Types of Motels

There are two types of motels: destination locations and those that attract people driving by on the road. The latter guests frequently do not make reservations ahead of time. Anyone interested in a motel as a second career should decide which type is preferable. Vacation places are often booked weeks or even months in advance, and the owner will have received credit card information and indicated back to the customer the motel's cancellation policy. Motels on the nation's highways—even those in vacation areas—are subject to the whims of drivers looking for a room. If you buy a roadside place and depend on people checking in late at night, you'll end up sleeping in your clothes.

It Is a Credit-Card and Not a Cash Business

Long ago the hospitality business was a cash-only business, motels especially. But in the past twenty-five years, it has become a credit-card-only business. The rates that owners pay the credit card companies vary but are around 2.5 percent for MasterCard or Visa and 3 percent for American Express. The benefit of credit cards to owners is that cancellation rules permit the charges to be billed. Credit card payments also provide better, more accurate record-keeping to owners of motels or B&Bs.

Insurance Payments Are Expensive and Mandatory

Liability insurance is costly and increases annually. You never know what type of accident or misfortune will occur on the premises, but one thing you can count on is that an injured guest will sue. Insurance payments increase proportionally if a pool or tennis court is part of the property. If food is served, as with a B&B, the insurance for health-related food service contingencies is necessary.

It Is Not a People Business

We hear friends say that we are in the "people business" but this is their warm and fuzzy fantasy. If the motel business is successful, the owners will see as few guests as possible. Check them in, check them out, and say thank you and good-bye. If you want to become involved with strangers and their problems, become a therapist.

It Is a Tough Business with Lots of Negatives

Here is our list of the major don'ts in the motel business:

1. Don't rent to proms or parties for teenagers.
2. Don't offer to rent to local housing authorities for the homeless.
3. Don't choose a motel with a pool. An owner will be a slave to the pool operation. Most counties require someone trained in CPR or pool maintenance on staff during all the hours the pool is open. This means that if you go out, someone with this training, whom you must pay, will have to guard the pool premises.
4. Don't negotiate with guests about the cancellation policy. If they have booked for the weekend and it rains, that's not your fault. If they are regulars who return each year, work out some extra free days for them the next season.

It Is a Tough Business to Sell

A B&B or small motel is difficult to sell. Frankly, there are not that many people, seniors or younger, who want to put in the time and effort to run one of these time-demanding businesses. If a working partner dies, such a business is nearly impossible to operate alone. When the need to sell is paramount, these are not the kind of properties that generate a quick sale from a large waiting list.

Other Ideas for the Would-Be Entrepreneur

The possibilities for becoming your own boss are infinite. The question is, what experiences in your past work can you build on in a venture of your own? Here are some of the more popular ways your retirement peers have found to turn that entrepreneurial dream into reality:

✔ Internet business
✔ Selling on e-Bay
✔ Consulting (a prime part-time occupation for professionals such as lawyers, business executives, and management specialists who leave full-time positions)
✔ Personal services

✔ Franchise operations
✔ Real estate sales

A cautionary note: Too often, the thought of easy money drives many people into ventures for which they do not possess the experience, time, or talent. We have seen too many bad self-starters who clung on for years, locked into an entrepreneurial fantasy, hoping against hope that future success was just around the corner. Sadly, they never knew when to quit and suffered great financial loss.

ReWorking Expert Advice

Finances and the Independent Contractor

Paul Piccone is a certified public accountant who has specialized in income tax returns for more than thirty years. His most important tip to people working for themselves for the first time is that they need bona fide income to use Tax Schedule C (Profit or Loss From Business).

He states, "Too often, individuals think that because they have started their own business, they are automatically entitled to deduct business expenses. But this is not the case if they generate no income from this new commercial enterprise."

Employees who work for companies receive a W-2 form at the end of the year. This familiar form enumerates annual income received and lists deductions from wages paid for federal, state, and city taxes, and the mandated contributions to social security and Medicare.

But when a person starts to freelance and work as an independent contractor on a project basis, monies received for these jobs are paid in gross sums without deductions. The wage earner is still legally responsible for all city, state, and federal taxes as well as social security. At the end of the year, the company that hired the freelancer will send a 1099 form, listing the total gross amount paid.

These are Piccone's recommendations for people who start to do new work as independent contractors so that they establish a tax and record-keeping system and maintain accurate records.

Have a different mindset as self-employed worker. As an independent contractor, you alone operate the business. You are its owner. The responsibility for recording expenses and income and making tax and other payments is yours.

Meet with a CPA or tax expert to understand the tax law and obligations, especially as regards 1099 income. Learn what payments to make and when. Importantly, discuss whether you should apply for a separate tax number for the business.

Work out a system to keep records. You need an efficient system to keep expense and income records during the year. Remember that all costs of running the business—such as home office costs, travel, and entertainment—are tax deductible. Keep all paper records and all receipts of purchases and expenses.

Maintain accurate records on a weekly basis. The local stationery store or office supply shop will have accounting ledgers. Or purchase a simple-to-follow computerized record-keeping system.

File quarterly. The IRS and your state have forms to facilitate quarterly payments of tax and social security. By paying these quarterly, you will not be left with a large payment obligation at the end of the tax year. Piccone's admonishment: "Too often, people see the increasing sum of freelance money and forget that they have mandatory tax commitments. The running income total needs to be reduced quarterly to reflect the business's obligations."

Open a business account at the bank. This reinforces the fact that you are running a business, and it separates business record-keeping from personal expenses.

Remit invoices for each assignment you perform as a contractor. You can make up a simple invoice form, or download one from the Internet. The invoice proclaims your professional status and indicates to the payee relevant information about your business, the specifics of the charge, and, importantly, either the newly acquired tax number or your personal social security number.

Meet with a tax expert to prepare taxes. Filling out Tax Form Schedule C will be a new and confusing experience for the first-time independent contractor with 1099 income. The smart move is to revisit the tax person who helped you when you first set up the business.

Working the Internet

The Internet's immense customer base of more than one billion people worldwide and its 230 million users in North America alone has become a siren's song to lure would-be entrepreneurs into business. Many think the Internet is a low-cost method for success.

Online, you will find many e-commerce services and offers, business advice sites, and get-rich-quick schemes. You'll find hundreds of sites that want to sell products or services or that offer you work at home for added, part-time income generation.

Many perceive that the easiest and least risky method of starting a business is by taking the e-commerce route. The Internet offers the convenience of working on your computer without leaving your apartment or house. However, it is easy to fall into the trap of spending hours on the Internet—ostensibly doing research or other activities supposedly related to your venture—and at the end of the day accomplishing nothing.

The truth is that doing business on the Internet is not much different from doing business elsewhere. You need definable goals, products and services, and profit. The main ways of making money from Internet operations are:

✔ **Sell a product or service:** Try to conceive of a product or service that will be in demand.

✔ **Sell advertising.** Essentially, you are selling what the industry refers to as "eyes," "hits," or "eyeballs." An advertiser who uses your site (perhaps it is a blog or provides useful information) pays each time someone clicks onto your site.

✔ **Link people to other Internet sites:** Your site is a conduit for people to seek information by clicking other Web site links or going directly to products. You act as commission agent for each link made.

A useful site for all of your Internet marketing questions can be found at *www.majon.com,* which provides practical answers to many of the basic Web site linking questions.

The start-up costs to mount a Web site are not prohibitive and can range from a few dollars for a one-page site with just text to a few thousand dollars or more to pay for an experienced Web person or company to construct a Web site with lots of bells and whistles. Also, there are many companies online or locally that can provide a variety of existing Internet design templates to fit your type of business at varying price points.

The question is, what do you expect to achieve with your Web site? And what amount of expense is reasonable?

Check with Yahoo, Google, AOL, and other Internet portals for minimum Web hosting costs. The credit card companies will charge you a percentage of each sale and then transfer these funds electronically.

Although the costs are minimal for a site, the fee only puts your site on the Web. Next you'll need to spend time and effort to move your site up the search ladder to as near the top of the search engine page as you can afford.

From your own search experience, you know that the first names that pop up in a search for products are often large companies. These top listings are shaded in light blue to attract the eye. The first and second positions are vital to major merchandisers. Interestingly, some large e-retailers control the two or three top positions on Google but not on Yahoo, or vice versa.

It is important to realize that unless the product or service is unique—a niche-oriented business—your Internet listing will be quite low on the search engine, and very few people will find it.

However, if you start a service business that relies on local trade or traffic, a Web posting will be helpful if, and only if, the searcher types in both the service and general location.

The Internet is a low-cost road to becoming an entrepreneur. Its added attraction is that running it can normally be done at home. But if you need income, establish a time frame when you'll fold operations and not throw good money after bad if the Web site does little or no business.

Consulting

Opening a consultancy firm is one of the most popular methods for seniors to work part time or full time, often in familiar occupations. It offers the potential for self-employment and independence, and the reward of operating a business and watching it flourish.

Many newly established consultants continue as specialists in their professions, having exited their companies for the freedom of working alone. By capitalizing on years of past experience (and past contacts), the consultant will have the best chance of success.

Most consultants cited autonomy as their greatest reward. There is also the pride in selling one's skills and not the reputation of the firm. On the converse side, the greatest stress in opening a consulting business comes in signing up new clients. This may become difficult to achieve if you try to compete with your old firm because often clients are reluctant to leave the familiarity and the support of a big practice for an individual. In your prior work, the sales force (maybe you were one of them) sold the service to the clients. Now, without that sales force in motion, where can you generate new business? And how soon?

Some people make good employees but bad consultants even when working in the same profession. Consulting requires the triple play of exercising people skills, serving clients, and generating ideas and projects. Many workers stated that at the beginning of their consultancy endeavors, a lack of refined and practiced presentation skills was the biggest drawback in introducing their services to prospective clients.

Those professionals who chose consulting as a work option for later in life should look first to their former company or organization for the initial consulting assignment. No one knows your work better than former coworkers and past supervisors. In many instances the goodwill you engendered in the years of working with these associates can be converted into new sales. Also, do not overlook old competitors as possible consulting assignments. They may be more interested in what you know.

The move to consulting necessitates a reassessment of past work habits and expectations. Here are the main concerns when working for yourself:

✔ You are the sole boss and employee.
✔ Lacking a support staff, you have to do everything, even the menial chores.
✔ You may be anxious about how to pitch the business.
✔ You must make all the sales calls.
✔ You may be discouraged by the lack of immediate sales.
✔ If you don't generate income right away, money is being paid out and nothing is coming in.
✔ You may be uncertain how to set up a business, pay taxes, perform financial record-keeping, and address legal concerns.
✔ You must determine how much to charge and how to charge it. (Do you want to work on retainer? Be paid upon project completion? Be paid an hourly rate? Who pays for your expenses?)

The primary disadvantage of a consulting service is that while you work on a new project, you must be pitching the next one. If you are not, this results in periods of feast and famine regarding income generation. Always keep a percentage of time for current projects and in the planting and seeding of new work.

What's Popular in Consulting?

Consulting works best when you do not need the money for living expenses. If people can find the occasional project and a small but loyal client base, there will be ample time to do the work and enjoy the extra income. It can become pleasant and flexible work that drains neither energy nor resources.

From our research, we found that the most popular types of consultancies for seniors are in the following areas:

✔ Technical and computer
✔ Management/business
✔ Career counseling/coaching
✔ Job placement
✔ Insurance
✔ Marketing/advertising/public relations
✔ Taxes/accounting
✔ Writing/editing services
✔ Personal services

The ReWorked Life

Women's Agency to Massage Therapist

For ten years, Julie Plummer acted as the director of Woman Care, a not-for-profit organization in north central Maine. The agency provided services for lower-income women in the region who needed clothing, food, shelter, and legal advice.

As Plummer approached her mid-fifties, she was burned out from the constant stress at Woman Care and started to search for a new career. She had undergone therapeutic massage after being injured in a fall and resolved to become a licensed massage therapist.

She decided on the six-month certificate program offered by the New Mexico School of Natural Therapeutics in Albuquerque, one of the leading schools offering a holistic approach to massage.

When she returned home, Plummer passed the test given by the National Certification Board for Therapeutic Massage and Bodywork. She was now licensed to practice in Maine

Plummer's initial marketing was to offer a free massage to residents living along her road in her small hometown. Some of the new clients worked at one of three nearby mills and praised her excellent massage work to others. Soon, after good word of mouth, she started building up a clientele from other people doing physical labor who needed relief from stress and pain. She said, "My relaxation and stress massages are like a treasure hunt to find the source of somebody's pain, and then bring it to an end."

Plummer continues to offer massage in her mid-sixties.

ReWorking Expert Advice

Becoming a Consultant

What many newly launched consultants do not realize at the outset is that time works differently when you have to both pitch and perform projects.

From our research, also, we found that some people went into consulting only because they had been laid off or terminated. They chose consulting as a last resort to generate income and not because it was a preference. Many expressed dissatisfaction with it. They were unwilling to give consultancy the time or effort for it to succeed.

As with any entrepreneurial venture, consultancies will experience the roller coaster ride of highs and lows of searching for and receiving projects and income. Often consultancy is a tradeoff, offering greater freedom and free time and less income generation. As with everything, you have to find a balance, but paying the bills comes first.

To learn about opening a consultancy, we turned to Patricia Dore. She made the successful transition from executive to consultant. After spending almost thirty years in the publishing industry, she left a vice president position at Scholastic, Inc. to begin Dore Associates in New York City. In the past four years, she has built a flourishing consulting business.

She shares the preliminary steps to the starting of a consultancy business.

Make It a Bona Fide Business

To set up a consultancy, you have to replicate the essentials of a bona fide business. Establish a separate e-mail address in some similar configuration as the business. At the bank, open a checking account in the firm's name. Also, it is smart to use a different address from your home for stationery, business cards, and labels (i.e., a P.O. box number or a suite and never an apartment address).

Visit an Accountant

Ask the accountant for a list of all the items that may be tax deductible for the consultancy. Keep records of these expenses, including meals, research of any kind, subscriptions, memberships, and costs for equipment, since they are essential to the business. Importantly, with the accountant do an expense spreadsheet analysis of what it costs you to live monthly, including operating the business. The monthly costs will represent the breakeven amount for the year.

Prepare an Office in Your Home

Dedicate a space in your home for an office with all the necessary business tools, including:

- ✔ Separate phone line (or cell phone)
- ✔ Computer
- ✔ Printer
- ✔ Fax
- ✔ Filing system
- ✔ Bookcases
- ✔ Stereo and television, if needed

One of the most surprising revelations is how much filing space a small business needs for keeping hard copies of reports, letters, research articles, and the like. Everything cannot be kept or filed on the computer. Find a reliable person for technical support—or, better, find two.

Write a One-Page Work Biography

Write up a one-page bio that summarizes what you can do for clients and that highlights talents, past accomplishments, and work history with case examples. You can include this with mailings or e-mails. It might be helpful to pay a professional for assistance in writing this.

Decide on Your Consulting Model

There are two kinds of consultants: those who propose something they can do for a client, and those who ask clients what they need. Whichever you decide—or even if it combines the two—write a personal note to all former clients and friends to announce the beginning of your consultancy.

If you are in the same city, request a meeting or set up a lunch. If it is too far to travel, set up a phone call. When you do meet, ask about projects for which the client might need help. Ask for leads on other possible clients, and be sure to inquire if you can use their names ("So-and-so suggested I contact you . . .").

Explain how you can help their business. Always write and say what a good meeting it was and thank them for the leads.

Develop a Model for Writing a Proposal

Write a short document in presentation form that outlines the assignment and its goals, and indicates how the work will proceed on each project. Also, mention how much time it will take to complete the work. Remember to leave time during the assignment for the client to get back to you, and time for you to look for other projects.

Figure Out How to Price the Work

It is best to charge on a project basis and not on time, but you need a sense of how much time it will take you. Gauge the range of fees a company is comfortable with, or if unsure, ask, "What's in the budget?" (Over time, you will perfect a better method for fees.) Another tip is to ask other consultants what they charge for their projects. You also need to create a simple invoice form.

Clarify the Scope of the Work

When given an assignment, follow up with a memo or letter citing the exact deliverable, the date, the method (written and/or oral presentation), and the timing of payments due to you. (Always try to generate one-third or one-half of the fee at the job's beginning.) Update your proposal and resend it with the final information.

Network, Network, Network!

Contact former and potential clients again every few months, perhaps to share some information about the industry. Or create a simple e-mailable/mailable newsletter about industry developments. Go to local conferences and seminars with copies of your work biography. Always carry business cards. Write to other consultants. Develop a network of noncompetitive businesses that can mention your name to their clients. If you meet with other consultants, brainstorm, ask for advice, and if possible, collaborate.

Know Your Work Rhythms

Establish a firm commitment to meet project deadlines. Over time, you will learn how to work efficiently. Suddenly you are obligated to set your own office hours. Can you work all night? Want August off? How many hours do you want and need to work? Keep records of time for each project, and discover how much you earned on an hourly basis by dividing the total time into the fee. Enjoy consulting; it is your new work life.

Franchises

Owing and operating a franchise poses another opportunity for people who want to be their own boss. Within the thousands of listed franchises offered across hundreds of categories, initial fees for start-up can be as little as $10,000 for tutoring services, or as high as many millions for a hotel operation.

What makes franchising so appealing is that it comes with both a proven system of business and a recognizable trademark. Think of the difference in traffic generation and brand recognition between opening a Ben & Jerry's as opposed to opening the first Gorman & Freeman's Ice Cream Shoppe.

The basic business relationship for a franchise is uncomplicated: the business owner or franchiser pays the franchisee a start-up fee to open an operation in a specific location. The franchiser will often provide training, assistance, equipment, and advertisements before the business begins. The seller of the franchise receives royalty payments, sometimes a percentage of gross sales or gross profits, and, frequently, an annual renewal fee.

The franchise seller will also provide marketing and research data on the most successful methods of opening the business and how to maintain a successful operation over time. The parent company also presents national advertising for the business, receiving a fixed extra amount of money from the franchisee for this specific purpose.

An excellent guide to franchises by types and to ranges of the down payment costs to buy a business can be found online at *www.entrepreneur.com*. Here click "Franchises" to browse the many types and learn how much each business costs.

We tend to be on the conservative side when it comes to retirement for seniors; we caution you not to deplete your savings to open an expensive franchise that will require a substantial capital investment up front. There are numerous books, articles, Web sites, and consultants that offer advice and warnings about franchises. You should err on the side of prudence before committing money.

Before becoming involved with a franchise, find out the failure rate of franchise operations of the type you're interested in. If this failure rate is high, ask yourself why you think you can succeed when others have failed.

Every person interested in a possible franchise operation should download the Federal Trade Commission's excellent guide "A Consumer Guide to Buying a Franchise," accessed at *www.ftc.gov/ bcp/conline/pubs/invest/buyfran.shtm*, or call 877-FTC-HELP to request the publication. You can also go to *www.ftc.gov* and peruse this site for other valuable business tips and publications.

Finally, a franchise is not only an investment in money but also in time. A person considering semiretirement may not want to put in the hours to operate a franchise business. Once the deal is signed, the franchisee is bound to operate the business in strict adherence to contractual conditions. The owner must maintain a good reputation for the franchise outlet because the parent company will not long tolerate an indifferent attitude to growing the business.

If possible, try to work in a franchise business that interests you. This will provide real-world experience as to what the business entails. Talk to other franchise owners. Nothing beats a real-world assessment from someone who has been in the business.

Personal Services

The vast field of personal services can include anything from tour guides to health-care givers to masseurs. This field will allow you to find employment that will probably come closest to being your hobby or avocation. These kinds of services often have flexible hours and are therefore ideal for older workers.

An important consideration is whether you need further training or education to start the personal service business. There are full-time courses at institutions and universities and many adult education classes. It is also vital to find out if you need to be licensed by the state to practice the personal service.

Here's our smart tip for opening up a personal service business: Consider serving the ever-increasing number of older baby boomers. Millions of people are turning fifty every year, and millions more will continue to do so for many years to come. As they age, they will require more services to support their aging lifestyle. This runs the gamut from tour guides to accommodate the escalating number of seniors taking bus trips and cruises to home care for the elderly who have need of personal services on a part-time basis.

ReWorking Expert Advice

Real Estate Sales

Selling real estate is one of the primary interests of people fifty years and older who consider retirement or arrive, finally, at retirement age. This is the type of entrepreneurship that many people consider when they think about retirement and future income generation. Selling homes seems interesting and exciting, the work appears moderately easy and pleasant, and importantly, it offers the possibility of good extra income.

How often have we heard, "I'm going to get my real estate license and work part-time when we retire to Florida, Arizona, New Mexico, or southern California"? Statistics indicate that when a housing boom occurred, as was the case in 2005—when home-buying prices escalated every month in all parts of the country—many more people applied for real estate licenses than usual. The prospect of cashing in on the lucrative commissions that came from selling houses in the million-dollar range produced a frenzy similar to the hopes and expectations that grow from buying a ticket for a multimillion Powerball Lottery. Everyone wanted a piece of the action.

Many Americans who want to work part time or full time in their retirement may consider a new career in real estate. Usually, these people have been through the process of buying and selling their own homes, possibly more than once, and perceive they have a firsthand knowledge of the transactional real estate process.

To demystify the experience, we asked seasoned real estate broker Mardee Cavallaro to provide her advice about considering the pursuit of a real estate license as a subsequent career in retirement. She has been actively involved in the business from more than twenty-eight years, having started out as an associate salesperson, and today is currently the co-owner of a northwestern Connecticut residential brokerage firm. (*www.BestandCavallaro.com*)

These are her tips:

It Is a Full-Time Job

Many people have the notion that real estate sales can be done part-time. This is untrue, and, in fact, it is very time-consuming. It also will involve coming in full days on weekends, and there is also occasionally some holiday work, since these are the occasions when buyers have the free time to drive around and examine the listings.

Also, new associates will be the people who must sit in the office mornings and afternoons in case some interested potential buyer stops in the office or telephones for an appointment. This is called "floor time" in the trade and usually involves either of two different shifts, one beginning at 9 A.M., and the second at 1 P.M., both lasting four hours each day.

Do Real Estate Locally

Sales in real estate are primarily a function of acquiring local listings most commonly in the town or county where you live. The better connected a salesperson is to the people within the community, the greater the opportunity of securing listings when these people decide to sell their homes.

Some believe that real estate sales stem from walk-in trade, and this is partially true of prospective buyers. But without ample listings (the supply), the buyer contact (the demand) will go begging for want of a large inventory of properties.

Acquiring homes to sell—the listings—represents the most important function of the real estate process. A person can be the best salesperson in the world, but without supply, few sales will occur. If you have listings, you have to contract with the seller and will be guaranteed at least part of the commission. With a buyer, you can always show other agencies' listings, but you will have no guarantee that the buyer will purchase a home through you.

The two rules of real estate are:

✔ Listings are the bread and butter of the business.
✔ Buyers are not always loyal to you.

Understand How the Commission System Works

Many people considering a new career in real estate hear the words "6 percent sales commission," the industry standard, although in truth the brokerage fee is always negotiable. They multiply this 6 percent against the sale of that $1 million home and come up with a gross commission of $60,000. (This leads some of the more naive to consider that one sale a year will generate all the added income needed.)

Here is the stark reality of the 6 percent commission. It will be sliced usually four ways. Most homes are co-brokered with two salespeople (buyer's and seller's agents) and that splits the fee, reducing the salesperson's commission to $30,000. The real estate firm will take its 50 percent out of the remaining $30,000, leaving $15,000.

This division applies not only to the nationally advertised brokers such as Century 21 but also to local brokerage companies with one office. There are also referral fees to out-of-area agencies that have recommend clients.

Sales Time Is Not Income Time

No one is paid until the deal officially closes. This can take many weeks or even months after both seller and buyer have agreed to the price. There are title searches, engineering assessments, financing, and other legal and financial considerations that must be met before the transaction is completed.

And the possibility always exists—no matter what the due diligence by both parties—that the deal will fall through. If this calamitous event happens, there is no sales commission.

The ReWorked Life

Oral Surgeon to Cartoonist

Dr. Dick Sebastian started as a pre-med student at Ohio State, but after two years, his advisor suggested that Sebastian start a dental program, beginning that course work in his junior year. Four years later with a dentistry degree, he was drafted into the army, served his time, and returned to Ohio State for three more years of oral surgeon study. Eventually, he and his family moved to Springfield, Ohio, where he established a successful practice.

Over the years, Sebastian started to receive competition from physicians whose medical school training now included oral surgical techniques formerly done mainly by dental surgeons. The result was that he was now sharing referrals with MDs.

With the fun and challenge of doing the more difficult oral work gradually diminishing, Sebastian decided at age fifty-five to access his IRA and retire to New York City. In Manhattan he started to take art and drawing classes at the New School and other painting and composition classes given by artists.

Sebastian possessed a fine wit and started to draw cartoons. His forte was watercolor dog cards, which he sent out during the holidays. Soon, friends and family encouraged him to try to sell these cards.

At the same time, a dog-owner friend recommended him as an illustrator to authors writing a humorous book on modern marriage.

In retirement, he actively paints and cartoons every day. And he is looking for a greeting card company to take on the line of

dog cards. Recently, he became one of the cartoonists for *www
.erugbynews.com.*

Solicit Friends for Listings

This is the second important part of the "do sales locally"
advice. Many new salespeople are reluctant to make this crucial
first step, and are doomed from the start.

If a person has a wide circle of friends and access to the community where he lives through local organizations (religious, civic,
athletic, etc.), this extended group can become the targeted pool
of potential listings. This first circle of contacts can and must be
widened to include friends.

Some individuals who have never sold real estate believe erro-
neously that they are acting pushy if they ask friends and family
for listings. The new salesperson will be content to make an initial
mailing and let the solicitation end there, hoping that the people
on his list will respond positively

Some feel embarrassed that they are making money off friends.
A few people think they will lose friends, who will become envi-
ous of the commission. But a novice real estate salesperson must
be proactive in asking (in a nice and professional way) friends,
family, and anyone else to give him their exclusive listings when it
comes time to put their houses on the market.

It Is Much More than Sales

A good real estate broker must develop the ability to match
the buyer's price range with a house that she can afford. Over time,
a broker becomes a surrogate therapist, almost a couples' coun-
selor, who must intuit the buyers' (when wives and husbands are
not in agreement) real needs in regard to housing.

A new home represents the largest single purchase in a family's
life, and buyers are often both unrealistic about what makes a
dream house and full of psychological problems in making a purchase decision. The agent must act as the go-between for buyer

and seller and, frequently, husband and wife. This part of the sale is artful negotiation.

Money Will Flow Out Before You Earn a Dime

The initial expense is schooling to learn the state's real estate statute requirements. Every state mandates a certain number of classroom hours from state-approved institutions or online. This schooling will cost about $300 to $500 but prices vary from state to state, depending upon the number of hours for class work. Some institutions in New York, for example, offer a three-tiered program: license study only ($250), license study and state exam prep ($350), and a deluxe program (at $425) for license study, state exam, and career counseling.

The next fee is for the license, which will cost about another $300 annually. Again, the cost depends upon the state. After licensing, a new broker must pay fees to join a local Multiple Listing Service and fees to join a local Board of Realtors. There will also be an outlay of expenses for promotion, advertising, and postage.

Finally, a salesperson will incur additional costs for maintaining a car. These include added gasoline, increased liability insurance for passengers, and the eventual decrease in the trade-in or sales value of a vehicle as it gains additional mileage. (Some people will also buy errors and omission insurance, which is usually paid for by the agency.)

You Can't Take It with You

For many retirees, the strategy is to become a real estate salesperson locally, do this for some years, then take the experience to the area of retirement and contract with a local brokerage house. This may not succeed as planned.

Think of all the other retirees who had the same idea. Certainly, within the retirement communities in the south they have sufficient real estate salespeople without need of any more.

When you arrive at the new retirement area, you are the newcomer without local contacts and without any listings. Why should a brokerage house want to bring on another new person? They do not. It is not a viable strategy.

Meet Local Developers

To my way of thinking, the only way for real estate salespeople who retire to new communities to have even a small chance at sales is to meet a new developer. If you have proven sales skills from having worked locally, the developer of homes, condominiums, or townhouses may want to bring you in as one of the resident salespeople on the new, yet-to-be-developed property.

In effect, you will be sitting on a large inventory of future listings. The commission may be less because of the captive nature of the assignment, but it at least will provide some income and introduction to the area.

Some friends who have retired to newer development areas in the two Carolinas and some of the Gulf States reported that they chose sites in relatively new communities with new development continuing. Most importantly, these areas were not inundated with real estate brokers.

Consider Commercial Real Estate

Commercial real estate is not as glamorous as residential sales and generates less income because it consists mainly of renting out space, although there is also the chance to sell a building. It takes a different kind of salesperson and a different mindset to be successful at this type of sales.

* * *

A Final Note

Opening your own business can become the realization of a lifelong dream. Finally, you are doing something that you enjoy, and making money from it as well. There is that great feeling when you can say (perhaps for the first time) "I'm in business for myself."

But go slowly at first to test whether the new activity—often stemming from a hobby or avocation—generates sufficient money and is the stimulating activity you imagined.

11 Volunteering

"Volunteers are the only human beings on the face of the earth who reflect this nation's compassion, unselfish caring, patience, and just plain love for one another."

—Erma Bombeck

The world of volunteering affords you almost unlimited freedom in your choice of occupation and the amount of time you want to devote to it. In addition, it is the one area of work where going online is the quickest and optimum method for finding and selecting the right opportunity. Finally, it offers the best and most varied employment opportunities for you to go abroad and work in an involving, project-based, philanthropic international activity.

Seniors want to volunteer. This is particularly true of those who retire and possess sufficient income to consider these kinds of assignments. Volunteering as the next career can fulfill your long-held wish to do that dream job or lifelong aspiration sidelined by working years in another career.

Some Smart Reasons to Volunteer

We have narrowed down the five most important reasons why you can and should volunteer. You may have other personal motivations based upon a religious, familial, or community reason. But the reasons listed below represent a realistic assessment of why this kind of activity is important to us.

It Occupies Time

We have placed time as the foremost reason because it represents a pragmatic assessment of the non-working daily life of a full retiree. You cannot garden or play golf, tennis, or bridge every day. Every day cannot be devoted to reading the latest fiction or non-fiction best seller or a mystery novel from a favorite author. Every day cannot be the slow wait for the early-bird dinner special to begin at 5 P.M. Volunteering motivates you to leave the house for many hours. It is a terrific way to go and spend time with new people who share similar interests. It is also time well spent without the past hassles and stress associated with work. In volunteering you can maximize negotiation for flexible work time. You set the number of hours or days you can volunteer. The agencies will accommodate these personal wishes but they will persistently demand more of your time.

It Contributes to Good Emotional Health

The act of volunteering clears away much of the inertia that affects those with nothing to do and no pressing financial reason to look for remunerative work. It accomplishes what work for pay cannot do: It inspires you to search for another activity that can be fulfilling, enriching, and done away from the house. If someone is financially set in retirement, there is no incentive to look for part-time work. Why would you want to go through the time-consuming activity of searching for a new job, taking an interview, and going to work if you did not have to? Why accept a job simply for a job's sake when it may not provide any emotional reward? Since income generation is not a motivating reason to do work, the act of volunteering represents the wholesome, do-good reason that can inspire you to shake loose from those long, repetitive days and weeks of monotonous inactivity. Although a person can resist looking for paid work, this psychological block fades when considering a chance to volunteer. Many will want to give back to the community.

The ReWorked Life

CEO to Language Helper

When Robert Greber gave thought to what he would do in retirement, one idea that pleased him was to learn to speak a foreign language. He had also wanted to travel and speak in the language of the country or area of his overseas visits.

Greber had enjoyed a long and diverse career in business, mainly but not exclusively finance. He had started out in the retail area of Merrill Lynch, eventually rising to be the resident vice president of the Los Angeles institutional sales office. In California, he became friendly with film director George Lucas, who hired him as Lucasfilm's chief financial officer after the first *Star Wars* film. Later, Greber advanced to CEO when Lucasfilm moved to the San Francisco area.

He bookended his career by returning to stocks and bonds but in a different fashion. He was appointed CEO and chairman of the board of the Pacific Stock Exchange, retiring after ten years at age sixty-one.

Soon after, Greber began to study Spanish intently and took the first of many trips to Guatemala for language immersion study. In Guatemala, he and other students lived for six weeks with a local family and spoke only Spanish.

While in Guatemala, Greber learned of Faith in Practice, a Houston, Texas–based not-for-profit organization that sponsored medical and dental missions to aid the poor of that nation. As a regular annual volunteer, Greber now acts as translator, interacting with the American medical staff and the local Guatemalan patients.

He plans to continue improving his Spanish language skills. This year his wife will join him in Guatemala for the first time.

It Is an Act of Altruism

Volunteerism is an act of altruistic service that helps others and—probably its greatest asset—helps the community. For those people who worked all of their lives in full-time jobs, prior occupations more than likely were about making money, getting ahead in the corporate or organizational world, and enjoying the benefits that came with such a position. Now, in retirement, these essential needs no longer exist. You can use old and new skills, often in some new and interesting activity, and feel good about it.

It Can Be Interest-Oriented

There are ample opportunities to choose a volunteer position that meets your special interest, whether it is teaching, health or medicine, working outdoors, tasks involved with children or older people, international affairs, politics, or vocational areas. This interest-driven pastime is one of the main reasons why volunteering is so attractive; it can become your avocation. For many retirees, the position dovetails with a particular pursuit or a hobby and is a chance to use personal skills for others' well-being.

It Connects You to Other People

The volunteer work will connect you to other people who share a similar interest or passion. It is a chance to make new friends or acquaintances.

Retirees often volunteer in pairs, deciding to choose a mutually agreed-upon service job. This keeps friendships, marriages, and other close relationships intact. Whereas two people might not agree on what remunerative job to do part time or full time, volunteering becomes the one way to facilitate remaining together.

What's Out There?

Volunteer positions exist from A to Z (Advocacy to Zoology) in every community and in every state and every country. The sky's the limit when it comes to choosing a volunteer activity. It might be helpful to list the vast range of possibilities for you:

✔ Animals
✔ Children and youth
✔ Crisis aid
✔ Disabled persons
✔ Education
✔ Employment issues
✔ Environment
✔ Health
✔ Homelessness
✔ Housing
✔ Hunger
✔ Immigration
✔ Law
✔ Medicine
✔ Politics
✔ Race
✔ Religion
✔ Seniors

Surely, among these many areas and others not mentioned, there is something of interest to everyone.

If you possess existing skills, they can be adapted immediately to any of these areas. Frequently, many not-for-profit organizations will offer some training to expand your proficiency.

ReWorking Expert Advice

Volunteering

What should you look at when deciding which organization would be most rewarding and decide how much time to devote to the project? All too frequently, you will go to work for the first not-for-profit organization you find or accompany friends to their organizations of choice. You will not give much thought to the reason for taking on the assignment. This is a bad way to choose your volunteering activity, since the options are almost boundless. You should find some work that really interests and excites you.

It is our contention that an individual should make the same detailed assessment of volunteer work as for a new part-time or full-time job. We asked businessperson Doug Fielding, president of The Companion Group, a leading retailer of barbecue accessories, to share his opinions on what seniors should consider before they start to contact volunteer organizations.

Fielding has been working for fifteen years as the unofficial urban expert in the San Francisco Bay area, advising amateur sports clubs on the best way to petition towns and cities to cede land for recreational development. In this capacity, he has developed knowledge about the whys and wherefores of volunteering from his own experience and from the experience of many other volunteers. He offers a practical assessment of volunteering.

Have Passion

If you like gardening and feel strongly about the environment, look at organizations that do creek restoration. If helping disadvantaged children is something you think has value, get involved in that area.

Do What You Want to Do

Using our example above, perhaps you do not really want to work one-on-one with a child but wouldn't mind working in a classroom. Or maybe you would prefer to work in an administrative capacity. Or it's possible that you only want to work one-on-one with a single child over an extended period of time. Make sure you are volunteering for something that will give you personal satisfaction.

Don't Bite Off More than You Can Chew

When a person initially volunteers, she is so filled with energy and enthusiasm that she often commits to many days and long hours. This experience can turn the act into a near-full-time job and bring back all the reasons why work became intolerable. Pace yourself. Learn to say, "No." Most volunteer organizations have an almost unlimited need for your time and will continue to ask you to do more and more.

Be very clear to the organization that you have time limits. "I can give you four hours a week. What would you like me to do?"

Find out whether it is better to work mornings or afternoons or after the necessary daily chores of life have been accomplished.

Keep in mind that even though you are donating your time, you're still making commitments to do work. If you have committed to help put in native plants by the creekside on Saturday, you aren't going to make many friends by deciding that morning that you just don't feel like doing the work because you are a "volunteer" who doesn't need to show up.

Find Out about the Organization

Do some preliminary research into the group you want to volunteer with. The best method is to contact someone who works there currently or worked there in the past. What do they like about the work? Do they like the people? Are the tasks interesting? Do they feel a sense of accomplishment?

Pair Up with Someone

No small part of the volunteer experience is being part of a community that you enjoy. Optimize the volunteer experience by pairing with a pal or a spouse. Another hint is to find an all-family kind of assignment. This can transcend generations and include grandparents, parents, and children.

Set Out to Learn Something New

Find an assignment that will provide a new learning experience. If you never worked with a computer, try to find a job where its operation will be taught to you. Many organizations will provide technical training. Or you can take an adult education or a local night course to acquire new skills that can immediately be put to use in the assignment.

Seek out professionals within the organization with whom you will be working and use them as experts in areas of your interest. This is especially true of medical professionals, doctors, and nurses. Use the volunteering opportunity as a useful means of discovery.

Enjoy Yourself

A large part of volunteering should be fun or provide you with a sense of purpose. If it turns into drudgery, go find another task within the organization or move to another group.

Governmental Opportunities

The U.S. government has five primary volunteer organizations, including the Peace Corps, and all are listed online under the banner of the USA Freedom Corps (*www.usafreedomcorps.gov*). If you go online, access its "interactive program selector," which will assist in matching interests, talents, and specific circumstances to the right agencies.

The government operates another Web site, *www.volunteer .gov/gov*, that offers many other volunteer positions.

These programs can be further investigated online:

AmeriCorps (*www.americorps.org*)—Created in 1933, this agency offers a wide range of programs to meet community needs in education, public safety, health, and environment. The two agencies soliciting older workers are VISTA and AmeriCorps State and National.

Citizen Corps (*www.citizencorps.org*)—Administered by the Department of Homeland Security, this agency's goal is to make communities safer and more prepared to meet the challenge from disasters. It liaises with state and community organizations.

Learn and Serve America (*www.learnandserve.org*)—Emphasizes learning programs for schools and communities, working from kindergarten through college.

Senior Corps (*www.seniorcorps.org*)—This is the prime governmental agency utilizing senior (that is, over fifty-five years old) volunteers. It runs three programs—Foster Grandparents, Senior Companions, and RSVP (the Retired and Senior Volunteer Program).

Each organization publishes booklets and pamphlets about its services. For more information, telephone 1-877-USACORPS.

The Peace Corps and You

The Peace Corps was established in 1961 under President John Kennedy's sponsorship. To date, it has served 138 countries with 182,000 volunteers.

Currently, it averages about 6 percent of volunteers who are older than fifty. The oldest volunteer in 2006 was seventy-nine years old.

It sends paid volunteers to seventy-five countries overseas in the following work areas: Education (34 percent), HIV/AIDS (20 percent), Business Development (16 percent), Environment (14 percent), Other (7 percent), Agriculture (6 percent), and Youth (3 percent).

A few additional facts that seniors should know before they decide to volunteer for the Peace Corps. You must be a U.S. citizen. The term of service is twenty-seven months with no shorter or negotiated term possible. The pay will be $6,000 received at the end of the term. A volunteer receives free medical and dental care. And only married couples (marriage license required) can volunteer together when both qualify.

Interested? Contact the agency at *www.peacecorps.gov* or telephone at 800-424-8580.

Volunteer.gov

This continues to be one of the best and most efficient Web sites to find volunteer work online. It is a well-organized, easy-to-use site that offers seniors a wealth of interesting positions; many of these are outdoors in the nation's woodlands trails or in federal forests. The partner list includes:

✔ Army Corps of Engineers
✔ Forest Service
✔ Bureau of Land Management
✔ Fish and Wildlife Service
✔ Geological Survey
✔ Department of Veterans Affairs
✔ National Parks Service
✔ Bureau of Land Reclamation
✔ Natural Resources Conservation Service, and
✔ Corporation for National and Community Service

Particularly helpful is that each job listed inside contains a full definition of the work, the length of time the volunteer will be needed, and the position's degree of difficulty. It also specifies whether seniors are eligible for the assignment.

Since many of these governmental positions are outdoors and seasonal, it affords the traveling retiree an opportunity to proceed cross country or north and south, volunteering along the way.

We have friends who are inveterate campers (and compulsive travel gypsies) who found the pleasures of offering their service to many of the out-of-doors organizations from the *www.volunteer .gov* Web site. Before starting on a long trek, they request the local telephone number and addresses of a volunteer organization along the way. Then they stop at a campsite nearby and contact the agency when they arrive. Each different stopover comes ready made with interesting volunteer work and new people to meet. Our friends keep active and enjoy contributing.

The Online Experience

Online has become the easiest method for seniors to investigate the many possibilities for volunteering. The search engine capabilities of each Web site can match people instantaneously after learning zip code information and a field of interest. Each site acts as a clearinghouse for volunteer positions.

This search method is present on all general sites, listing positions within twenty miles of a volunteer's zip code. One click moves inside the particular organization where further information can be found about the type of job, address of the organization, and telephone number.

For those with a more specific concern, preference in location, or request for a type of organization, the optimum search method is to type in the word "Volunteer" followed by a second search word. For example:

✔ Volunteer Rhode Island
✔ Volunteer Catholic Charities
✔ Volunteer Environment
✔ Volunteer Hurricane Katrina
✔ Volunteer Africa

This method will winnow down the search and bring up agencies that can accommodate the specific request.

For seniors without computers or Internet access, the public library will provide contacts and instruction on locating volunteer positions.

VolunteerMatch.org

VolunteerMatch (*www.volunteermatch.org*) is the effective one-stop search for all volunteer positions in the United States, not including those offered by the federal government. This is the number-one online site for the nonprofit sector, the most accessed by people who want to volunteer.

It serves millions annually, providing a single source for 40,000 nonprofit organizations, including the American Red Cross. Tens of thousands of people view it daily.

The ReWorked Life

Importer to Civic Hero

Douglas Fielding studied urban planning in graduate school at the University of California–Berkeley. Afterward, he decided to remain in Berkeley, a place with a national reputation for a proactive city council.

After eight years working for a public policy consulting firm, he opted for a career in business. While living in Berkeley, he coached his daughter's soccer team and eventually became president of the 3,000-member youth soccer league. Gradually, as he approached fifty years old, he began spending more evenings involved in the development and expansion of soccer opportunities for young people and adults interested in the sport.

He realized that the critical barrier to meeting the increased demand for recreation was the lack of field space. The most important task was to find land and to petition city councils to authorize development for new sports fields. From his work in public policy and business, he understood how to organize people to overcome resistance from city councils to purchase land for non-revenue-generating recreation.

His interest turned into a part-time avocation, and he became a specialist in field development. Last year, he could say with pride that through his efforts nine playing fields were made available at a cost of $35 million.

At age fifty-seven, Fielding continues to play in a pick-up seniors' game of soccer every Sunday in the first field developed in Berkeley—which is called, appropriately, Fielding Field.

Other Online Sites

Other well-known volunteer organizations online are also very useful and efficient in linking seniors to volunteer assignments.

Volunteers of America is at *www.voa.org*, and United Way is at *www.national.unitedway.org.*

We also recommend SCORE, an excellent business volunteer organization; it is America's premier source of free and confidential small business advice for entrepreneurs. The agency has helped seven and a half million business owners. It is located online at *www.score.org.*

Many of our associates from the business world have opted to work for this organization, to give back much of what they learned about business. Like so many other national organizations, retirees who spend part of the year in the Sun Belt can find SCORE branches throughout the United States and continue to serve while living in vacation homes.

Volunteering Abroad

Seniors who want to volunteer abroad will have the option of short- and long-term international assignments, but both kinds require the volunteers to pay expenses for travel, meals, and lodging. With an extended stay of two or three months or longer, airfare and other charges can run above $6,000. Most international volunteer assignments are of shorter duration and cost less than $1,000.

This pay-as-you-go format differentiates volunteering in the United States from positions out of the country. Within the wide range of opportunities and countries are some programs that can be three months in length and others that are a week or less. In effect, the latter might be considered short-term travel opportunities with some environmental interest (e.g., whale watching).

These volunteer overseas opportunities combine an individual's interest in doing good with the prospect of living in another culture. Teaching English is the primary activity, easily managed by all volunteers. All programs include medical and travel insurance, food (three meals per day), and assistance from local staff upon arriving.

The two organizations with long-term and successful track records for overseas assignments are Projects Abroad at *www.projectsabroad.org* and Cross-Cultural Solutions at *www.crosscultural solutions.org*.

On the Projects Abroad Web site, you can investigate the costs by clicking "Prices." But remember, the country-by-country tariff menu does not include airfare, which is also listed.

Additional online international organizations to look at are:

✔ The Association of Voluntary Service Organizations at *www .avso.org*, which provides links to volunteer work for and through European organizations
✔ Idealist.org at *www.idealist.org*, which operates a database for 68,000 nonprofit organizations throughout the world
✔ International Volunteer Programs Association (IVPA) at *www. volunteerinternational.org*, another clearinghouse for many not-for-profits around the world

To summarize, international assignments are limited to people who can afford these trips. Through this kind of volunteer work, you can fulfill a life goal of traveling to other countries and helping people in the Third World.

The ReWorked Life

Tire Executive to PGA Volunteer

Englishman John Hoffen began working for the French-owned Michelin Tire Company in the United Kingdom in 1956. The company wanted to expand into the high-end tire market in the United States, and in 1963 it sent Hoffen to its New York office, which numbered a mere forty-five employees. Sales that year totaled about $10 million.

For the next thirty years, Hoffen assisted Michelin's spectacular rise in U.S. tire sales, so that by 1993, when he retired, the company had increased to 26,000 U.S. employees and almost $7 billion in domestic business.

At first Hoffen, aged sixty, resisted retiring full time and started as a consultant in training and reorganization of sales organizations. He worked on a semipermanent basis with a company called Hewitt-Coleman in Greenville, South Carolina, a third-party risk management company.

Hoffen had been playing golf since age thirty-five and is a member of the Green Valley Country Club in Greenville, South Carolina. He helped to organize the club's first senior golf group among older members, recognizing that these retired men wanted to keep active by playing golf and participating in friendly competition with other senior golfers at other clubs in the area.

Fully retired from the business world, he found an outlet for his organizational skills by volunteering as a marshal for the United States Golf Association. This involved performing crowd control on assigned holes at various tournaments. The highlight for him was volunteering at the 2002 U.S. Open Golf Championship at the famous Bethpage Black, Long Island, course. He hopes to continue assisting local tournaments in South Carolina.

ReWorking Expert Advice

Volunteering Abroad

Tom Pastorus operates the American branch of Projects Abroad, one of the most successful and dedicated organizations placing people overseas in volunteer assignments throughout the five continents. Since 1992, this organization—originally founded in the United Kingdom—has offered a diverse range of teaching, care, conservation, medical, journalism, and work projects, plus the opportunity to live with and become an integral part of a local community abroad.

Pastorus has witnessed the significant increase in U.S. volunteers wanting to do work overseas, particularly among people over fifty years old. His advice is to do extensive preliminary research to find a bona fide organization through which to set up international volunteer work. Be realistic about expectations.

He said, "Seniors will invariably inquire about a 'comfort level,' which is a catch phase for the type of living accommodations in the Third World. Too many people have a naive assumption that underdeveloped areas may offer similar amenities as in the States. When they discover, too late, this is not the case, it spoils their first days. But when they become accustomed to the conditions, they do fine."

Volunteer opportunities abound for people who want to do good in another country. Many seniors are reluctant to make the kind of long-term commitment demanded by the Peace Corps' two-year obligation. In most cases, service abroad will entail some out-of-pocket expenses for travel.

These are the most frequent questions Tom Pastorus is asked.

Q. *What are the opportunities for seniors to volunteer for international work?*

A. There are many opportunities, particularly in the areas of education and working with children in orphanages.

Q. *Can couples go to the same place?*

A. Yes, we can always accommodate two people who want to go abroad together. With two people, there is a better chance of finding a higher-class living facility. On occasion, two may opt to pay for a more modern habitat.

Q. *Can people choose a country or an area?*

A. Again, yes. We find lots of volunteers who know some Spanish and request Latin America or South America. These are the kind of volunteers who have already made plans to travel in that region after their work for Projects Abroad.

Q. *Are global opportunities increasing?*

A. More and more countries are looking for people, and now even European nations see the benefit of English-speaking and dedicated volunteers. More countries are signing on with us to help them find American volunteers.

Q. *Is the demand being met for these global positions?*

A. Not entirely. Our organization has seen a substantial increase in volunteers in just the past few years, many more applicants coming from people over fifty. After serving abroad, many people return with an appreciation of their stay and offer positive word of mouth to friends back home about the overseas experience.

Q. *What are some of the unrealistic expectations?*

A. Privacy, comfort, and cleanliness. Often times, people have to share a room with another volunteer. The food is always different from American meals. Basically, it is not what your mother made, and some people have a difficult time getting used to the "foreignness" of the situation.

Q. *Do some project areas dominate?*

A. Teaching is the primary placement, and orphanage work is second. Many people also want to do environmental projects. We do turtle watch assignments in South America and Asia, rain forest conservation in Peru, and big game park internships in South Africa.

Q. *What are things to check on when going abroad with an organization?*

A. 1. Is insurance included in the stay?
2. How many staff members does the organization have on the ground?
3. How much is the travel cost and how is it paid?
4. What is the cancellation policy?

Q. *Are all volunteer abroad organizations alike?*

A. No. Projects Abroad insists on a one-month minimum commitment. We can extend the stay to two or three months. But some other organizations are more geared to short-term volunteering and will offer a weekend or one- or two-week junkets.

Q. *What do you see in the future for volunteering overseas?*

A. We predict many more opportunities with more choices of countries. Also, we're finding that people who go for two months invariably take the third month to stay in the country and sightsee. By then, they know the language and the customs and really have a terrific time.

The ReWorked Life

Editor to Museum Docent

Carrie Rosenthal enjoyed a long career as a copy editor at *Reader's Digest* in Pleasantville, New York, rising to become a senior editor. She resigned after her husband was transferred to run a publishing company in Atlanta. After the move to Georgia, she continued to work on occasional assignments from the magazine.

But the freelancing work was sporadic and did not fill up the days. In her mid-fifties, Rosenthal did not want to return to full-time employment and started to look around for volunteer work. In one of Atlanta's free newspapers, she spotted an advertisement for docents at the Michael C. Carlos Museum at Emory University.

Rosenthal knew that docents act as knowledgeable guides to escort groups through the museum, explaining the exhibits and answering questions. It seemed like interesting and educational work. She applied and was accepted.

The museum provided six months of training about its history, permanent collection of artifacts from the ancient world, and helpful hints on how to lead visitors through the space, particularly groups of children. One facet of the training was that new docents enrolled in Art History 101 given at Emory University.

Today, after ten years of docent work, Rosenthal averages a minimum of six tours a month for groups of children and adults. In addition, Emory University offers its docents the perk of auditing classes free with the permission of the instructors, and she has taken fifteen undergraduate courses in Art History, Classics, and Philosophy. Rosenthal considers docent museum work the ideal volunteer job: educational, collegial, and enlightening.

New Ventures in Volunteering

As more Americans enter their fifties and sixties over the next twenty years, not-for-profit organizations are coming up with innovative ways to harness their work experience.

A pilot program that looks promising is called ReServe Elder Service, which can be thought of as volunteer work for pay for older adults. It connects older, educated seniors with volunteer jobs that pay a modest monthly fee. These stipends act as an inducement for seniors who want to volunteer but need extra income. Currently, the pilot program is based in Queens, New York. If successful, this interesting idea of senior pay for volunteer assignments could expand to other parts of the country.

For more information about the progress and the opportunities, go to *www.ReServeInc.org*.

Local Search

We have left the most obvious method of volunteering for last—working in the community through neighborhood organizations. The best-known organizations are the American Red Cross, Boys and Girls Clubs, the Salvation Army, and the United Way.

Within your town or city are thousands of volunteer opportunities that exist locally in religious institutions, hospitals, senior citizen centers, youth programs, scouting, civic organizations, and countless others. These can be found in the Yellow Pages under "Social Service Organizations." Here are some of the possibilities:

✔ Literacy programs
✔ In-school assistance
✔ Teen emergency centers
✔ Crisis centers
✔ Shelters for battered women
✔ Foster grandparents

The ReWorked Life

District Manager to Street Patrol

Dave Poster ran the New York office of Wrangler Jeans for twenty-four years. As he entered his late fifties, he began to look seriously at retirement, embarking on an annual assessment of income needed to exit the company and stop working forever.

He calculated a safe investment number that if reached would suffice to cover his household, medical, and discretionary expenses. When he reached age sixty-one, the monthly statement from his investment broker arrived, and he was delighted to see that the number had been reached. He gave notice that day.

Years earlier, Poster, a resident of Greenwich Village, New York, attended a community meeting to meet the Guardian Angels, a youth crime-fighting patrol. The group had been asked to patrol Village streets where the quality of life issues had deteriorated because of drug sales and prostitution.

Poster became a member of the Christopher Street Patrol, an auxiliary group that accompanied the Angels on their nightly rounds. Over time, the dual patrols successfully reduced crime in the neighborhood.

He liked the feeling of doing well for the Greenwich Village community. When he retired permanently, he devoted more time to the patrol, eventually becoming its president.

He actively sought out more local volunteer groups. Currently, he is a member of the thirty-two-block Greenwich Village Block Association and of the Community Emergency Response Team, started after 9/11.

Poster's civic work fills his week with activities.

* * *

A Final Note

Volunteering can be psychologically rewarding, and it lends itself to individuals who have time on their hands. There is also the reward of knowing you did something good for another person or your community. However, many volunteer opportunities bring you face to face with other people's personal misfortune and tragedy. You may be cut out for that or you may not. You can't save the entire world, just a small part of it. Be honest with yourself about what volunteer activities will suit you over the long haul. It may be a worthy cause, but if you find yourself going home anxious and depressed, it is time to look for another organization or mission to serve. There are a myriad of ways to contribute.

12 The Retirement Community

*"Retired is being twice tired . . . first
tired of working, then tired of not."*

—Richard Armour

A retirement community can be a treasure trove of work opportunities for those people who plan to retire to a new location or for those who remain in the same area. The potential work can be entrepreneurial or salaried, part time or full time, a conventional job or one geared to an older population.

Income can be found more easily in newly built retirement spots. Those states, such as Florida, Arizona, or New Mexico, that have been attracting retirees for decades do not offer as many promising opportunities as such states as Georgia, North Carolina, and South Carolina, which have recently started to interest retirees. This fact might determine, ultimately, where you decide to make your last move.

Facts and Trends

Research predicts that about one-third of all workers reaching the age of retirement will make plans to move. This could be a change to a smaller house or apartment in the region where they live or a move to a retirement community or retirement area in the same state or out of state.

Since the 1950s the warmer states have witnessed the arrival of millions of part-time and permanent retirees. A high percentage of current and future retirees will forgo remaining in their native states and instead will head to the traditional Sun Belt areas of Florida, Arizona, New Mexico, and southern California.

Recent housing statistics indicate that those states not previously selected as retirement areas are experiencing booms in houses purchased by new retirees. Developers in these states are buying up large tracts of land to construct more retirement homes.

Las Vegas and its outskirts are the prime example of a surge in new building activity, to welcome both new retirees and younger families. The city grew from 852,000 inhabitants in 1990 to 1,563,000 by 2000, much of the growth from seniors seeking affordable retirement living in a warm climate. Builders complete a new home every twenty minutes as 5,000 people move to Las Vegas every month. And with the surge in population, service industries, shopping malls, and medical care follow, creating new jobs.

Many northern-based seniors do not build homes in these warmer states but instead rent apartments and condominiums for a month's stay or more in the wintertime. These renters swell the senior population for a short season. But while they are there, they need the same services and care as full-time residents.

Searching in the Retirement Community

You should consider retirement locales potential areas of untapped opportunities to find work with other seniors as clients. Some retirees focus the search for work (paid or volunteer) where they live; they should redirect that search if they have plans soon to move to a retirement area.

Before considering a work search in the retirement neighborhood, take time to reflect on the differences and opportunities that these communities offer, some of which may not be offered in non-retirement areas.

Determine which retirement communities are older and settled. Those locations will have already established a service economy that serves the local population. The probability of new part-time and full-time work will be substantially greater in emerging, newly built communities that have not been tapped yet by other businesses or services.

There are three types of retirement housing:

Retirement Communities

Retirees often buy, build, or rent houses in areas that offer such amenities as golf, tennis, and beach or mountain facilities. Some of the just-turned fifty-year-olds buy today to retire at a later date. The older crowd has already decided to move here, most likely full time. The community may have been in existence for many years (e.g., Hilton Head, South Carolina, or Boca Raton, Florida) or may have been more recently developed (e.g., St. James, North Carolina, and all the Sun Cities developments).

Retirement Areas

People will buy, build, or rent a house or an apartment in an area (state or location) that is known mainly as an area that attracts retirees. These people either remain the year round, or vacation in the winter months (they're known as snow birds). Examples are the entire state of Florida and Santa Fe, New Mexico.

Same State

Retirees who opt to stay in the same state—many to be near children and grandchildren—may not have the breadth of opportunities to find work among other retirees. However, by being clever in their search, these people can also target senior communities where they live.

The ReWorked Life

Financial Planner to Professor

I'm Bob Gorman, one of the authors of this book. I started to work in the insurance business after serving for three years as an officer in the Navy. Over the next thirty-five years, I rose from salesperson to regional branch manager to positions in senior management for such well-known insurance companies as Phoenix Mutual, John Hancock, and Provident Mutual.

In my late fifties, I began a series of financial seminars in New Jersey for people over fifty years old. During the question-and-answer part of each meeting, I learned firsthand the interests and apprehensions of seniors about their financial future.

In regard to my own retirement, I made two long-term decisions: to build a vacation home in eastern North Carolina, and to try to become an adjunct professor at the University of North Carolina–Wilmington. To accomplish the latter goal, I first applied for and was accepted at New Jersey's Gloucester Community College, where I taught Management.

I contacted UNC–Wilmington, and using the experience at Gloucester as a springboard, I was assigned to teach Marketing and Management courses. I'm happy to give back to these college students the years of real-world learning from my successful financial services career. It helped that I had an undergraduate degree from Brown University, an MBA from Iona College, and many professional honors and degrees.

Finally, in my sixties, I partnered with my college roommate, a business writer, and am the coauthor of this book, *ReWorking Retirement*.

What Work Is in the Planned Retirement Community?

Planned retirement communities must offer a menu of amenities to their residents. Whether the community features huge tracts of land and enormous homes or connected townhouses with recreation rooms, it will still require people to provide products and services to the population beyond the permanent labor force that maintains the facility.

Frequently, these communities are built in rural areas, and that means the region does not have a sufficient resident population to serve the needs and habits of the newly arriving retirees. Many northern urban and suburban dwellers want to replicate some of their eating and shopping preferences in the new southern areas where they live. This demand creates businesses.

Some of the needs within these planned communities are:

✔ Telephone operators
✔ Bookkeepers and accountants
✔ Hosts and hostesses in the dining rooms
✔ Beauticians, hair care, and barbers (doing in-home work)
✔ Financial and tax advice
✔ Travel planning
✔ Sales
✔ Receptionists
✔ Maintenance
✔ Security

Our friends who have moved permanently to these types of communities have told us that each one offers a bulletin board where members post needs and wants. Most retirement communities frown upon your using their e-mail listings to solicit work or sell services. But some will allow you to post searches for work or products to sell on the main bulletin board.

Finding Opportunities in the New Communities

Let's suppose you need to find part-time or full-time work. You've chosen a new area that has been recently developed. Immediately, you notice that the infrastructure is lacking many products or services that the new arrivals will want and need. How do you take advantage of this situation?

This presents a golden opportunity to begin a start-up business. Here are some of the services that will be required by arriving retirees:

✔ Interior decorator
✔ Computer and technical support specialist
✔ Tree, flower, and shrub specialist
✔ Exterminator
✔ Massage therapist
✔ Nutritionist
✔ Physical therapy
✔ Airport limo service
✔ Photographer
✔ Relocation specialist

Initially your business may only have a few clients because the development is new. But as housing development expands, so will your client base. This will afford you an increasing supply of clients with potential for more growth as the neighborhood expands and additional seniors arrive.

The Settled Retirement Area

It is more difficult to begin some entrepreneurial activity in a retirement community or area that has been in existence for many years. The new retiree becomes yet another financial planner or caterer in a community that has a sufficient number of these businesses.

The best way to look for work in an established community is to present your skills to companies or firms that do business in the vicinity and employ retirees. Most need a continual supply of experienced new workers owing to existing worker mortality, retirees moving permanently into assisted living or nursing homes, or the inability to work flexible hours as their health deteriorates.

It is also smart to visit these companies before you decide to settle in a community. Again, if securing work is vital to paying your costs, the promise of a job in hand is worth more than a long and futile search for meaningful employment in an area already crowded with others whose skills are the same as your own.

Some baby boomers plan to retire based upon availability of employment or the prospects for starting a business in that area.

For these people, income generation becomes the number one variable (other than climate) in determining where to settle.

The ReWorked Life

Executive Assistant to Dog Walker

Ann Driscoll raised five children in Connecticut then began a career as an executive assistant at Bombardi, manufacturers of airplanes, where she worked for fifteen years, earning a small pension. She retired to eastern North Carolina when she turned sixty-five.

There was a small gap between her income and expenses, specifically medical costs, which tended to escalate each year as she grew older. She began to work at the basketball games of the University of North Carolina–Wilmington, earning a minimal hourly salary.

She realized that it would be difficult to find flexible-time work as an executive assistant in the shore region of North Carolina. She was forced to look for other ways to earn income to meet her expenses. But she puzzled over what she could do at her age.

Then by chance, friends in the retirement community asked her to dog-sit while they went away and insisted upon paying her a per diem fee. Driscoll did not want to bring the animal into her own house and instead agreed to care for the dog at the client's home.

Soon after, her dog/house-sitting service was spread via word of mouth in the small community, and other clients requested the same service. Not only were their dogs well cared for; someone was watching out for their homes.

Driscoll realized that since many people could not travel with their dogs, she had found a profitable and enjoyable niche business. She calculated a fair price for sitting one dog and a higher fee for taking care of two dogs.

A surprise bonus was that grateful clients also provided for her meals in their homes while they traveled.

Finding Work in Retirement Health Care

Health and living care present the best possibility of employment for retirees seeking work with other retirees. Growing numbers of the aging population need part-time or full-time care.

Naturally, medical personnel will be welcome with open arms in the communities where they retire, and if you are a health-care professional you should be able to arrange flexible work hours. This is particularly true for skilled nurses and clinical technicians. It also includes people with medical and hospital administration experience and workers who possess medical bookkeeping and data entry knowledge, especially of the intricacies of filing Medicare and insurance forms.

Within assisted-living facilities or nursing homes, you can find interesting jobs that do not require specific experience. One, for example, is program coordinator, a person who plans and implements events and activities for the live-in residents.

A relatively new service is professional health insurance filing and medical bill paying specialists. These people take care of a person's medical payments, often earning a percentage of the savings they find in the bills.

Other Health-Care Jobs

Other, lower-paying positions offered by the health-care industry are:

✔ Resident-care assistants
✔ Administrative secretaries
✔ Food preparers
✔ Food servers
✔ Housekeepers
✔ Janitorial staff
✔ Groundskeepers

Many of these positions come with health and dental insurance, 403(b) tax-deferred retirement savings, flexible hours, a credit union, and paid time off. Most offer one or possibly two free meals a day.

Even part-time workers who do not qualify for health insurance may be offered benefits such as paid time off, tax-deferred retirement savings, theme park and local golf course discounts, jury pay, and bereavement leave.

If a retiree needs just a small amount of money to pay bills, a job in a health-care facility can be a great way to generate income.

Tips for Tapping into the Community

Upon arriving in a retirement area, the retiree with something to sell or market to the community should take these steps:

1. **Set up a Web site.**
2. **Print business cards.** It is simple and easy to do at home. Template forms exist at all the chain office supply stores. Start to carry these with you always.
3. **Check with the community board about what's allowable for business canvassing.** Posting hard-copy notices on bulletin boards? Classifieds in the local newsletter? Notification in the online Web site? Using the e-mail list for solicitations? Find out what's permissible.
4. **Get a copy of the community directory.** Most planned communities have an address directory of the residents. This can be the prime source for an introductory mailing. Write a short and informative letter, citing what your product or service is and your years of experience. Enclose a business card.
5. **Place a classified ad in the community newsletter announcing your new business**, or find a *Pennysaver* or its equivalent.
6. **Join a local business club.** If you were a member of Rotary, Elks, or Kiwanis, join the local branch of these service organizations. Back home, these were good sources of leads and contacts, so continue using the groups in the retirement area.
7. **Sponsor a local event.** To maximize awareness upon your arrival, sponsor an event with a local business. You could cater

a barbecue, arrange a wine and cheese tasting with the local liquor store, or offer to pay for a pail of golf balls at the local driving range. The key is to introduce yourself and your business to as many potential customers as possible. A contest with a prize offering is also another way to publicize your presence.

8. **Run a seminar or give a free lecture on a topic.** This can range from financial and tax information to nutrition and health-care concerns. Offer a written leave-behind with name, address, telephone, and e-mail address. In retirement communities, the pace is more leisurely, and residents will welcome an informative presentation on a topic of interest. Be sure to watch the cost of the occasion and remember that seniors will neither drive at night nor stay up for a late evening event.

9. **Network.** It remains the best way to generate new business.

Some Caveats about Working the Community

It is important to be persistent and goal-oriented in looking for work, but many communities have strict rules about businesses run within their boundaries. These restrictions mainly apply to strangers (i.e., your clients) coming in and out of your residence. But there may be also codicils that prevent an active, visible business from operating at all.

It is understandable that a steady stream of strangers coming and going would both disturb the community and create some apprehension. This is particularly true in connected townhouses or apartment complexes. A solution for the businessperson is to find or share office space away from the complex.

Don't be overly aggressive. The community exists because people have come there to relax and retire, so you do not want to come across as an obnoxious, high-pressure person whose only interest is in making a sale.

Strategic Partnerships

Try to find out who runs businesses that serve the community. Gather their business cards and sort these into two piles: those that can help your business and those that cannot.

If possible, introduce yourself and your business concept to all other enterprises that seem to be helpful and noncompetitive. Make sure you indicate that you will reciprocate their goodwill.

A tip that worked well for some is to invite a group of business people for cocktails. This will be especially beneficial if no such network exists. You'll be remembered as the person who brought everyone together.

The ReWorked Life

Book Writer to Web Creator

I'm Allyn Freeman, the other author of this book. I've enjoyed many different careers, flitting from one to the next in a constant challenge to reinvent myself. No one job, no one occupation has remained constant during the forty years in which I alternated between the creative and the commercial. One employer called me "a bohemian in a button-down shirt."

I first worked in Paris as the European representative of a U.S. textile company, was employed as a product manager of a New York City electronics exporting firm, and owned and managed a restaurant in Manhattan. All this before turning thirty.

I then worked in four different advertising agencies on the account management side after having received an MBA in Marketing from Columbia Business School. Seven years later, I headed to Los Angeles to write television episodes of *M*A*S*H*, *Hart to Hart*, and other television shows.

I returned to New York and worked as a consultant for a natural body-care company, was an executive in a firm doing political research, and did freelance writing for business newsletters.

Then I began writing business books (*Why Didn't I Think of That?*, *The Leadership Genius of Alfred P. Sloan*, and this book, *ReWorking Retirement*). In addition, I started Freeman Global, a consulting firm that specialized in making appointments in the United States for European economic development agencies from Navarre, Spain, and North-Rhine Westphalia, Germany.

In 2006, when an old friend from my rugby-playing days asked if I could create and provide content for a new Web site (*www.erugbynews.com*) and become the Director of Business Development for the company, my answer was, "I'm available."

* * *

A Final Note

Time and again, retirees have told us that it is the early bird that catches the worm in generating business within a new retirement area or community. Many of the people we interviewed said the principal mistake was waiting too long to embark on offering products or services. By the time they were ready to launch a commercial enterprise, it was too late, and other retirees were well on their way to success.

Another question in working the retirement area or community is, does your spouse want to join you in this business? Couples who retire will spend more time together than when one or both worked careers. It's important to share the same opinion on an agreed way forward in starting a business in the retirement community. The consequences can be negative if only one person is interested in this new activity. Our advice is that you not put a strain on your marriage by overworking a new business idea.

See if your company operates a branch near an area where you would like to retire or where you vacation for the winter months. This will present you with an excellent opportunity to work flexible time, generating income and still enjoying leisure time. We have a friend, a mechanical engineer in his seventies, who chose a particular Florida location precisely because his company had opened an office in a nearby city. For the five months he and his wife are in the Sunshine State, he goes to work two or three days a week. The company is delighted that it retains his engineering skills.

13 Senior Women

*"Most women are one man
away from welfare."*

—Gloria Steinem

We include a separate chapter on women's opportunities to work in retirement for two reasons: First, the historic inequality in pay between men and women continues to have a negative impact on women as they age and work. Second, many senior women will face the horrible specter of poverty and will therefore have to work well beyond age sixty-five.

All statistics—taken from the U.S. Census Bureau, the Social Security Administration, the Administration on Aging, and other institutions—confirm that older women are more likely to be poor than men. One example: in 2003, 10 percent of Americans age sixty-five and older lived below the poverty level, but 71 percent of these were women. There are increasing numbers of elderly women who have no other option but to find some kind of work to maintain even minimal subsistence. Older women in financial need have become a significant subgroup within the senior population. This aging female segment will enlarge as boomers continue to retire. And this depressing trend of elderly women enduring poverty and hardship can be expected to continue at least for the next ten to fifteen years.

More recently, the U.S. Census data from 2005 revealed that women over age sixty-five were more likely to live in poverty (less than $9,367 in annual income) than men over the age of sixty-five. Statistics show that many women in this age group suffer extreme financial hardship. Some elderly women cannot maintain basic housing or sustenance needs. This growing subclass of females in poverty is at significant risk of falling through the safety nets of federal, state, and local agencies.

Living costs escalate annually for seniors, who must sustain housing, property taxes, and food, medical, and drug costs. Will we soon see pitiful images of elderly women swaddled in blankets and dropped off by children, grandchildren, or well-meaning friends at nursing homes and hospitals like unwanted babies?

It is vital for all women to understand the prospects of retirement and to be mindful that working may represent the only means to make ends meet in later years.

Senior Women

Although women in the boomer generation are significantly better educated than women who preceded them—and currently enjoy better pay and greater benefits than their predecessors—societal, cultural, and gender factors will have an adverse impact on retirement of all women, college educated or not.

Data from the Bureau of Labor Statistics indicate that women fifty-five years and older are continuing to work in high numbers. The Bureau stated that in 1996 only 49 percent of women aged fifty to fifty-four worked full time, while in 2006, this rose to 65 percent. Of greater significance is that in 1996, only 32 percent of women sixty to sixty-four worked full time; that increased to 45 percent by 2006, the first year the baby boomers turned sixty years old. This 13 percent gain reflects the factors of divorce and debt. It could suggest that that many of these women had no other choice but to stay employed. But it could also indicate that more women have careers they enjoy and don't want to leave.

Factors Affecting Women in Retirement

Diverse socioeconomic factors form the reasons why women in the United States face potentially perilous financial futures as they age. The customary system of putting money aside to be taken out in later years has produced an inequitable result since women in the United States have never experienced the earning capacity of men nor, on average, spent the same amount of time in the work force due to time off for raising families. Among the reasons why American women are at a disadvantage are:

Longevity—Women in the United States on average live nearly eighty years. This will increase in small increments over the next twenty years. Extended years will necessitate continual income.

Longer life expectancy than their spouses—Because men's average life expectancy is only seventy-five years, married women face the probability that they will be widows for some time. This could mean lower social security benefits in instances where both husband and wife worked all their lives and collected the maximum upon retirement. A widow in this scenario will see her household income cut in half.

Depleted savings—The family nest egg will suffer significant losses if the woman must pay for an older husband's nursing or medical care or if she herself has hefty medical bills.

Divorce—The substantial divorce rate has left many women living alone without a second spousal income. In addition, many women who faced divorce in their forties or fifties entered the labor market later in life without the equivalent work experience or education of males who began careers in their twenties. This belated entry allowed women less time to participate in the pension plan.

Interrupted careers—Many women opted to take time from their careers to raise children. The mommy track reduced their chances for earning the same large salaries and bonuses over time as males with similar education and career skills. When these women did return to the labor market, their incomes were lower and the potential income levels were reduced by the years out of the work force.

The ReWorked Life

Medical Writer to Contractor

Karen Kolbert studied art and design in college in the United States and continued her artistic education in Italy where she met and married an Italian. The couple lived in Naples where she became fluent in the language.

Friends suggested that with her proficiency in Italian she should teach English as a foreign language. She recognized that the most immediate needs locally were courses for the medical staff at the University of Naples. Later, she saw a unique opportunity and wrote a book titled *English for the Medical Profession*, the first of its kind in Italy.

Some years later, now divorced, she returned to New York City and was hired as an adjunct professor to teach English as a second language at Manhattanville College. She continued to teach ESL for a number of years.

When she turned fifty, Kolbert embarked on a six-month cross-country trip, a subconscious exploration for the next place to live. She liked New Mexico and decided to move to Santa Fe.

She was determined to discontinue teaching, and while she considered what else to do, she decided to build her own house. Costs would be lower if she became a general contractor on the project. Then, she studied and passed the real estate exam and received her broker's license.

Today, Kolbert is part of a successful Santa Fe real estate brokerage firm, performing sales duties.

Smaller pensions and benefits—The entire system of benefits and pensions is based upon earning capacity. Women who worked fewer years than men have put fewer dollars into all private and federal benefit systems, meaning that they will take out less money upon retirement. The gap between expenses and income can only be met by continuing to work. (Social security data reveal that one-third of women will receive benefits based upon their own earning histories.)

Traditionally lower wages—Today, according to the Bureau of Labor Statistics, women earn nineteen cents less per dollar than male counterparts. While this is better than 1969's thirty-seven-cent inequality, the wage disparity will continue for the fifty-five-year-old woman up to the time she stops working full time.

Higher tax rates for married women—The government regards a woman's income as the second income "stacked" onto the male's wages. In effect, lower-income working women are taxed higher (in joint incomes) for their labor, lowering their financial reward from working.

Husband's earlier retirement—Generally, women are younger than their spouses. When a husband retires, the wife often does so as well so the couple can spend time together. The result is that females check out of the labor force at a younger age, sometimes giving up high-paying positions and not further advancing their business skills and incomes.

Husband's earnings—Many wives did not pursue full-time work or careers because their husbands were the major breadwinners. This is especially true in households with large financial assets.

In addition, many wives have remained in the dark about life-long family income, and have allowed their husbands to make financial decisions. One issue that often affects women is the choice of the pension option. This typically offers three choices:

1. **Life income only**—Gives the greater pension dollar amount so long as the husband remains alive. On his death, the pension ceases to exist.

2. **Reduced lifetime amount**—Offers two-thirds of the maximum amount as long as the husband or wife is alive. Payments cease only when both are dead.
3. **Life income 50 percent**—While the husband lives, couples receive 70 percent of the maximum amount. Upon his death, his spouse receives 50 percent for her lifetime.

The law requires wives to authorize in writing which pension benefit they will receive. But many women sign without understanding that it is possible pension benefits will either disappear when the husband dies or be significantly reduced.

Women age fifty-five and older will return to the work force in lower percentages than males in the same age segments. Women will also earn less, a carryover from a lifetime of earning inequity and reduced social and financial incentives to work.

Preplanning for Finding Work

Women, whether single, married, or widowed, must consider work as they approach retirement. They must understand what economic fate awaits them in the years ahead, especially those women who have always deferred financial decisions to their husbands.

Senior women should think of working in retirement as both a generator of needed income and as an insurance policy to help cover health and medical problems that may affect their spouse or themselves. A woman who can plan effectively for the future has a better opportunity to avoid the pitfall of inadequate income to cover living expenses in retirement.

What to Do?

For the millions of women who worked part time or not at all during most of their lifetimes, a smart move is to consider some kind of training today for higher-paying work tomorrow. This could mean a return to college to finish a degree, embarking on technical training to learn computers, learning a trade via internship positions, taking classes in operating a small business, and other schooling that can provide a new skill base to qualify for remunerative work.

If not higher education, then women should seek out apprenticeships in trades that might interest them. This could be cooking classes, paralegal study, or other training that can certify them for a position. Women actively apply for and are often hired for the intern positions that appear frequently across the job spectrum.

Some women we interviewed started to consider future occupations at as early an age as forty-five. Some attended law school, some went to nursing school, and some acquired a master's degree in business administration. All realized that a profession would enable them to find higher paying work, which they could continue full time or part time into their sixties.

An excellent Web site for women of low and medium income is that of the Women's Institute for a Secure Retirement (*www .wiser.heinz.org*), which offers basic information aimed at helping women assume financial control over their lives. The site has advice on retirement, financial counseling, and other issues helpful to women.

Work Searches Online

Women achieve some small benefit from having their own online job search companies that deal exclusively with females looking for work. Federal and state discrimination laws prohibit mentioning gender in work ads or notices.

For female seniors looking for work, online searching is a mixed bag. Such searches are easy to activate, but they lack many of the benefits of using recruitment and placement firms. Networking provides the best opportunity to find the next job, and it is better than any services provided by online search firms.

Many companies with Web sites will request that you submit a resume online. This is often the proper and first way to assess candidates and their skills. Do not confuse this with online job search companies that, sometimes demand payment for posting resumes on their sites.

The ReWorked Life

Hospital Worker to Volunteer

Ann Miller Patch exemplifies the scope and variety of volunteer work that can be accomplished by the energetic and interested female senior. She found that by doing some preliminary investigation before retiring, she was able to narrow down the choices of volunteer possibilities.

When she turned sixty-five, she began to consider the options of retirement from her career as a clinical therapist. The initial step in the transition process was to reduce her workweek from five days to four. For the first time in twenty-one years, she enjoyed the pleasure of scheduling repair and delivery appointments during a weekday at a time when she was home.

On this day of no work, she also started to explore the local options for volunteer work. She recognized that when full retirement came at age sixty-six, she wanted to be busy during the week.

Patch settled on two volunteer jobs after a few months of networking and exploration. The first one was with the American Red Cross, which realized that Patch possessed two skills important in its disaster relief efforts, a clinical background and acquired Spanish-language skills from language immersion lessons in Costa Rica.

The second position came from the National Association for the Advancement of Colored People, which needed work on an archival project, collecting and categorizing the history of the Maine chapter. Patch had no background in this specific area, but the NAACP recognized her organizational and managerial talents.

She is busy in retirement, alternating time between the two organizations and planning additional Central American trips for more language instruction.

Women's Jobs Online

That said, there exist many online job placement sites geared solely to women. Among the women-only online sites, we found that some posted many job listings throughout the country and some put up only a few. Further, some demanded an annual payment for placing resumes on the site so they can be downloaded and reviewed by employers. A few others asked for a monthly fee for posting resumes and providing updates on new positions posted. We say, caveat emptor—buyer, beware—when it comes to paying for these placement services.

All Web sites we found appeared to be for professional, career-oriented women with no separate feature to appeal specifically to women age fifty and older. Among the sites:

✔ *www.WomensJoblist.com*
✔ *www.WomenForHire.com*
✔ *www.Careerwomen.com*
✔ *www.ForHerSuccess.com*
✔ *www.Feminist.com*

Most of these Web sites will allow you to search by field of interest (e.g., Advertising, Retail, Financial, etc.) and location (state and sometimes city or a maximum radius of miles away from the work location). The number of positions posted is directly proportional to how many companies use the site to list jobs (and many of these listings frequently are generated by third-party recruitment agencies).

Are these jobs reserved exclusively for females? Absolutely not. It would be illegal for companies to post positions for any group in regard to race, age, or ethnicity. Do these positions exist on other job sites? Probably.

These sites also publish tips and hints on finding jobs and provide suggestions for advancing in the workplace. Some operate seminars that travel throughout the country lecturing on issues affecting women in the workplace. We suggest that you examine each site and see if it's helpful to you.

Specific Online Job Sites for Women

If a woman has a particular talent in some professional field, she can find online sites that cater to this expertise. Some of these positions are offered through associations or organizations, and on occasion you will need to join (for a fee) in order to access the job information on the site.

A handful of these sites are:

✔ *www.WomensSportsJobs.com*
✔ *www.WISCNetwork.com* (Women in Sports Careers)
✔ *www.NWSA.org* (National Women's Studies Association, a site that specializes in not-for-profit work)
✔ *www.WomeninConsulting.org*
✔ *www.NAFE.com* (National Association of Female Executives)

These Web sites for women are not the primary method we recommend for finding a job but, since so many exist—in numerous professional categories—it may be worth a look, especially if your talent or wishes corresponds to a certain professional group.

Nontraditional Jobs

The U.S. Department of Labor lists jobs that are nontraditional for women—that is, jobs in which women made up less than 25 percent of the work force (e.g., airline pilot, electrical technician). Some other possible nontraditional jobs for senior women are:

✔ Chefs
✔ Barbers
✔ Clergy
✔ Office and computer repairpersons
✔ Chiropractors

A dedicated Web site, *www.Work4Women.com*, helps women of all ages explore work in nontraditional areas, listing training and support systems. Interesting information can be found also at the U.S. Department of Labor's Women's Bureau ("Quick Facts on Non-Traditional Occupation for Women") that will provide a complete list. Go to *www.dol.gov/wb*, click Statistics in the right-hand column, and scroll down to the bottom of the page.

The ReWorked Life

Lawyer to Nanny

Patricia Clarkson's high school class in the late 1950s had the highest percentage of students accepted at college of any public school in its state. Yet, out of the hundreds of women from this school who went on to university, Clarkson became the class's only lawyer after having worked in and been disappointed with the low-level jobs given to females in the country at that time.

Clarkson passed the Maryland and Washington, DC, bars, and then the Florida bar when she and her family moved south. When her children reached middle-school age, she started as an attorney for a law firm, juggling the legal work with family commitments.

After a number of years of full-time employment, she scaled down the law work to devote more time to her family and children. She also started to do pro bono legal work, much of it domestic law for indigent women in the area.

Many years later and in retirement, with her children married and settled, Clarkson has been called on to do full-time granny work for her older son's six-year-old boy. Her son and his wife have a new baby and needed someone to serve as the playmate of the active and curious youngster.

She now spends afternoons and weekends shepherding her grandson from one activity to another. Finally, she has the full time to give over to exploring museums, zoos, batting cages, miniature golf, and many cultural events. As the grandson ages, she will again do pro bono legal work.

Sales Is a Good Option

Sales has been cited before in this book as a relatively easy field to enter, offering the possibility of immediate employment and the opportunity to make substantial income. Most sales entry-level positions do not need hours of coursework or licensing examinations. The main exceptions are real estate and stockbroking, both of which call for extensive study to pass licensing examinations, often from specialty schools.

For women who need immediate income, sales can be the optimum method for finding good wages. In addition, sales jobs are the easiest to locate. The classified section of most town and city newspapers is filled with ads seeking people to sell goods and services.

Sales books abound on the best techniques for successful selling. These can be found in the Career section of most bookstore chains but also every public library offers a selection of sales books.

There are a wide range of selling possibilities:

1. **Retail:** Mass merchandisers and chain stores may offer fair wages, medical coverage, pension, and probably no commissions. During the holiday season retailers always add on people, and working during this period can give you a preview of what the job and the income would be like full time.
2. **Telemarketing or telesales:** Small wage, generous commissions are characteristic of these types of sales jobs. However, it can take a long time and many calls to make a sale. Moreover, many states and the federal government maintain growing lists of people whom telemarketers cannot call.

3. **Direct sales to consumers:** These jobs entail face-to-face contact to sell somebody something. This may be any type of goods or service including health and life insurance, financial planning, house care (burglar alarms, lawn care, termite protection, etc.). Generally, the pay is a salary draw against commission.

4. **Direct sales to business:** The customer is a business or firm in need of items for the upkeep of a plant or office. These items may be office supplies, computers, copiers, coffee machines, desks, chairs, lamps, industrial cleaners, software systems, employees, etc. Pay is a salary draw against commission.

5. **Party plan:** Tupperware, Southern Living, Pampered Chefs, other in-home sales products. There is a commission on sales.

6. **Real estate:** Commission is split between the salesperson and the real estate company following a sale.

The better the salesperson, the higher the income.

A Final Note

Women who retire must solve the problems that come from living longer than spouses and earning less over a lifetime. This is particularly true for those pre-boomer-aged women who have less education and fewer years of higher-paying work experience. It will be up to women themselves to work out innovative solutions to find work and income in their later years.

14 Foreign Opportunities

"All of life is a foreign country."

—Jack Kerouac

Some Americans will consider retirement from the old career as the opportunity to look for work overseas or start a business in a foreign country. These people fall into two groups: those who consider this a novel experiment and will continue working for many years in a new business abroad, and older retirees or semi-retirees who are looking for a different life experience, moving to some other country other than the United States.

Going abroad offers both promises and problems, especially in a country where the language is not English. There are often cultural differences that dispel American's romantic notions about time and place. And, for older retirees, health and medical concerns must also be considered, particularly for seniors on Medicare, which, as a rule, does not cover foreign hospitals or foreign doctors.

A relocation abroad can be tonic to those willing and able to make this kind of move. And there are many citizens who were born in another country, retained their familial language skills, and returned to the nation of their birth to retire or to begin businesses, using their American career experience.

We anticipate that there will be a gradual upsurge in retirement communities in those foreign countries where the costs of living are substantially lower than in the United States. We do not mean Western Europe or Japan but rather many other developing countries, particularly Central American nations. As more people choose to relocate in countries that are affordable—and form expatriate communities—a corresponding need may arise for services and products that you can provide.

Today this retirement overseas concept is in its infancy. Only Panama offers and advertises opportunities for retirement in that country. But for the retiree who is fifty years old today, the future may present many new opportunities in other countries that see the potential of luring Americans.

Saving money is the primary reason why some Americans move overseas. The factors behind this phenomenon are twofold: the perception of a lessened ability to live well in the United States on social security, savings, pensions, and rising medical costs, and lower living expenses aboard. Americans see the possibility of getting more for their money in a foreign country compared to housing, food, and medical costs in the United States.

Another reason to go abroad is the prospect of adventure and the lure of a foreign lifestyle.

Caution: The Social Security Administration has a list of which countries can receive direct deposits abroad and which cannot. To check on the status of all foreign countries, go to *www.ssa.gov/international.* The SSA will not send monthly payments to Americans who live in Vietnam, North Korea, Cambodia, and Cuba, and this list may expand depending on the future political situation.

Reduced living costs overseas may preclude having to find a post-retirement job or remaining locked into an existing one. The savings generated from the lower costs of living in some of these other countries may mean you won't have to dip so deeply into your retirement income and savings. Daily living expenses and housing costs are lower for many developing countries.

One person we interviewed said, "I decided not to continue working in North Carolina, so I built a home in Mexico, and I shall never work another day. I give golf lessons locally for free, and this covers my greens fees."

As more Americans opt to go overseas, the greater the possibility for work to service this burgeoning expatriate community. Some potential areas for entrepreneurs will be investment and tax advice, banking, and legal services.

Will Americans retired in Costa Rica or Thailand develop a yen for bagels or doughnuts? You could be the person who supplies this community with familiar American food products.

Americans who work abroad are still subject to U.S. taxes. However, in 2006, money earned exclusively in a foreign country was excluded up the first $80,000 made from non-U.S. earnings. This benefit is another incentive to retire aboard and work. There are two tests to qualify for the foreign-earned-income exclusion:

✔ A home on which taxes are paid in a foreign country
✔ Meeting the Internal Revenue Service's residency or physical presence requirements

Check with the IRS and your accountant about changes in this rule and other factors affecting foreign income for American working abroad part time or full time.

Finally, many countries require visas for extended stays.

ReWorking Expert Advice

Living and Working Abroad

Rick Consodine saw an entrepreneurial opportunity years ago and now operates a new business in Ireland, which has become a spectacular place of new business growth. During his time in the United States, Consodine had worked in sales, spending thirteen years with IBM in office products, then another eleven years in commercial real estate, and finally another eleven years as sales manager of Photo Systems based in Michigan. This is Consodine's story, as he answered our questions about work and retirement in Ireland.

Q. *How did you choose Ireland?*

A. My wife and I made thirty-seven prior trips to Ireland before we decided it would be a good place to buy a house. After all those visits, we were familiar with the country, its people, and how everything worked. We bought a house in 1988 in Galway when I was forty-eight. At that time, I had not given much thought to what I would do, if anything, in retirement. All I did know was that I would end up in Galway.

Q. *What business idea did you conceive of for Ireland?*

A. Naturally, when you live abroad you take a lot of the American systems of business with you. One day, we needed to store some items and I realized that there were no self-storage facilities in Galway, a city of 100,000 people. We wondered whether self-storage would be a good business. Could the concept be introduced to the Irish?

Q. *What did you do next?*

A. I called a friend in Ireland, who had been the attorney when we bought the Galway house. He thought self-storage was a promising idea and offered to invest the seed money if I built and operated the facility. Within a month, I resigned from Photo Systems and traveled to Las Vegas to learn about self-storage, Ironically, I arrived back in Ireland to live full-time on St. Patrick's Day of 2003.

Q. *What happened after you arrived?*

A. We built a 100,000-square-foot self-storage facility about two miles from Galway's city center and started to advertise its availability. It did not take long for the residents to realize the benefits of placing items in storage. Many of the old houses here are small, and the facility proved a great convenience to eliminate clutter inside.

Q. *What about the currency exchange?*

A. Ireland is part of the European Union, which uses the euro (€) currency. The dollar is currently worth around $.78. What this means is that our social security payments in dollars, when converted to euros, have a 28 percent less buying power. On the converse side, I earn income in euros from the storage facility and receive about $1.38 for the dollar conversion when I return stateside. Because we're back so often, it probably evens out over the year on a one-euro-for-one-dollar basis.

Q. *How do basic living costs differ in Ireland from the U.S.?*

A. The standard of living in Ireland has improved dramatically in the past twenty years thanks to new investments and a prosperous economy. Dublin is now one of the most expensive places to live in the world. But I would say that the costs between the two countries are even, with some prices for local produce less than in the United States (and the items here are fresher, also). In the supermarkets you can find almost all items sold in America, including premium American ice cream. Gas is more expensive.

Q. *What about medical costs?*

A. Our medications in Ireland cost about $115 per month. We took out local health insurance that comes to about $1,500 for the year. The health care in hospitals is very good once you are admitted, but often that critical part is not always that easy. We have a wonderful general practitioner in the nearby village of Ballyvaughan, who would match any family physician we met in America.

Q. *Name some benefits and lifestyle experiences in Ireland.*

A. There are no real-estate taxes, but high income taxes. Liquor is quite costly and a pint of Guinness is approaching $4.00. We belong to the Galway Bay Sailing Club, and I am active in the

Galway Chamber of Commerce. Ireland is not for the sun-seeker. The weather is unpredictable, generally a bit cool and rainy, with just enough sunny hours to keep two former New Englanders happy.

Q. *What advice do you have about Ireland or living abroad?*

A. Rent a place for three months to see how you like it. Come back again in another season to experience a change in climate. If it is not Ireland or Great Britain, I would recommend language immersion courses to become familiar with a different language. Key also is what sort of medical and health systems are available to a foreigner. Here in Ireland, we see the new building of more apartments. A person can rent a charming, four-bedroom place for around $1,000 to $1,250 a month, plus utilities.

Q. *What about your retirement?*

A. I have not yet retired at age sixty-seven—I intend to "semi-retire" in about three years. At that stage, I plan to spend about half of my time on each side of the Atlantic, probably in two- or three-month intervals. I will work with the self-storage in Galway on a part-time basis. But also when back in the U.S., I intend to do some consulting for storage companies interested in expanding in Ireland.

It all worked out better than I anticipated. I did not have a plan to start a business when we bought the house in 1988, but that's the wonderful fortune of living overseas.

Medical Considerations Abroad

Health and medical care are the dominant concern for those who choose to move to a foreign country. When qualifying for Medicare at age sixty-five, seniors will not be covered in overseas medical institutions.

Here is the specific Social Security statement: "Medicare generally does not cover health services you get outside the U.S. The hospital insurance part of Medicare is available to you if you return to the U.S. No monthly premium is withheld from your benefit payment for this protection."

This medical limitation may influence your decision about retiring overseas and subsequently looking for work. There will be no pending medical dilemma if you have sufficient income to pay for doctor visits locally, pay for medical insurance that covers foreign care, or purchase medical insurance within the country.

U.S. medical insurance brokers are developing products and portfolios to offer you policies before going overseas. If the demand increases in the more popular retirement areas, some of these brokers may open offices in these same locations. These offices could provide work opportunities for those over age fifty who are retiring abroad. Other issues to consider:

- ✔ The additional or supplemental cost of local medical insurance plans to be used only within that country
- ✔ The quality of the total medical infrastructure (physicians, hospitals, ancillary care)
- ✔ The ease of finding and seeing qualified doctors near the retiree's community
- ✔ The ability to communicate with doctors in English
- ✔ The difficulty of being transported back to the United States for emergency procedures or life-threatening illnesses

Many newly written international medical policies have different amounts of time you are allowed to spend back in the United States for care (e.g., thirty days, sixty days). If you are in good health and have annual procedures such as colonoscopies, CAT scans, or PET scans, stent treatments, and the like, you can continue to have these done in the United States with these maximum-stay medical insurance policies.

The ReWorked Life

President to Sons' Business Overseas

Finbarr Murphy was born in Ireland and met his American wife, Christina, in Basel, Switzerland, more than forty years ago. At home, she was involved in running the USA Weleda, her family's old-world pharmacy in New York City, which sold European natural body-care products and anthroposophical medicines.

Murphy realized that the health-food business in the United States was starting to grow and moved the Manhattan pharmacy to Rockland County, where he started to manufacture more of the natural baby products, shampoos, soaps, and body lotions. Murphy became president and witnessed the company's growth from a small pharmacy into a multi-million-dollar entity. Under his leadership, Weleda USA expanded into quality health-food stores throughout the United States.

In 2002, Weleda, Europe, the parent company, bought out the shares of the U.S. subsidiary. The Murphys decided to retire to Dingle, Ireland, on the west coast, where the movie *Ryan's Daughter* was filmed.

He made an important financial decision to take his retirement package from Weleda, Europe, in euros and not in dollars even though it was a one-to-one ratio at the time. He had greater confidence in the stability of the euro than the dollar.

In Dingle, he encouraged his two Irish-American sons to open the first premium American ice cream company, beginning with a retail store in downtown Dingle. The company has expanded into supermarkets throughout Ireland and has also opened a second retail store in Killarney.

Murphy is fully retired, spending time learning Gaelic and acting as a financial and marketing consultant to his sons.

Panama, the Overseas Retirement Standard

Panama has become one of the foremost countries to attract American retirees. Some predict more people will either investigate this country or make plans to relocate there than any other. To date, the country has acquired an excellent reputation as a place to retire, as favorable articles have appeared in the *New York Times, International Living,* and AARP's magazine.

Panama has become attractive for two reasons: its infrastructure and governmental support for the influx of retirees. As stated, Panama will, very likely, set the benchmark for other countries looking to attract American retirees.

A few of the main reasons why Panama is popular:

Climate—Located about nine degrees north of the Equator, Panama enjoys a pleasant, year-round warm climate.

City, mountain, or shore locations—It affords the retiree different lifestyle choices for relocation.

Stable, friendly government—No worry about civil disorder. Panama is a historic partner with our government.

Dollar is monetary unit—The dollar is legal tender in Panama, so there are no exchange problems or unfamiliarity with the currency.

Property purchase—Americans can buy and own land without any restrictions, receiving the same rights as Panamanians.

Inexpensive local labor—Panamanians earn about $1.00 minimum wage.

Health care—There are numerous U.S.-style health-care facilities serviced by English-speaking doctors, many of whom were trained in the United States.

Tax exemptions—The government has suspended many import duties on construction materials, importing household goods, etc.

Language—English is extensively spoken.

The media spotlight shines positively on Panama, and the small country will see record real-estate development as retirees come from the United States and from Canada. Other countries are studying the Panama model.

Finally, we're confident that the success of Panama in providing new work opportunities for retirees will establish the standard for other retirement communities abroad. When the media follow up on retirement life in Panama, we believe they will record many new entrepreneurs who have opened flourishing businesses and services geared to the expatriate community

Overseas Jobs

If you buy a vacation or retirement house in a foreign country, you can keep active and employed through three main types of work abroad:

✔ Teaching English
✔ Volunteering locally or through an international or American organization
✔ Running an entrepreneurial venture

The possibilities of starting a self-owned business abroad are many and varied. One tip is to view the community with "American eyes," to look for gaps in businesses that exist in the States but are not yet in operation in that country. Some countries have license requirements that apply to all residents. It's always helpful to seek some preliminary advice from a local attorney.

Foreign Rates of Exchange

Most foreign countries offer you the option to buy or build homes. For the most part, these are individual houses or apartments, and not part of any planned U.S. retirement community.

In the United Kingdom, Ireland, and many western European nations, the cost of living is equal to or higher than the United States. Costs are greater because of the decreased buying power of a weakened dollar pegged against the euro or the British pound. In effect, dollars buy about 28 percent less in Europe at 2007's rate of exchange.

For those seeking to work in western Europe, being paid in euros is a boon because there will be no currency exchange loss. Further, those Americans who earn euros will receive a favorable rate when they exchange the euro for dollars on return trips to the United States. Foreign exchange rates are quoted daily in many American newspapers, and can also be found online.

One last statement about Western Europe: The latest and most advanced medical techniques and procedures exist in almost all of western European countries, and many physicians and technicians came to the United States for high quality medical training.

* * *

A Final Note

If considering retirement overseas, you should make a careful exploration. Talk to someone who has already made the decision to live abroad, and ask all the important questions. Make a preliminary trip to that country and find other Americans there. Repeat these questions to everyone you meet. An intermediate step is to stay a few months and try to imagine what it would be like to live and work in this country for most of the year. For the just-turned fifty-year-old who will consider retirement five or ten years later, it is helpful to keep up-to-date on retirement trends overseas.

The exchange rate of the dollar is one of the key economic variables subject to change in the future. If, for example, the dollar rises significantly against the euro, the cost of living in Europe will fall dramatically.

Finally, in the future, when visiting a country that you might consider retiring to, always keep an eye out for what kind of work, if any, you could do there.

15 The Future

*"I did not say the future could be
foretold but I said that its conditions
could be foretold."*

—H. G. Wells

What will the future bring? What might be different in your life
five years, ten years, or twenty-five years down the road?

One thing is certain: Just like today, you will be concerned
with money and meeting the costs of living. That is why so many
boomers insist they will keep working in some capacity past their
formal retirement. Factors such as uncertainty about social security payments, steadily rising medical costs, increasing longevity,
and the need to stay employed and connected for health and well-
being will keep fifty-, sixty-, and seventy-year-olds in the work
force.

The good news is that there will be more working opportunities for older workers over the next decades. This will come from
two events: companies and organizations will alter present procedures to allow you to structure flexible work schedules and, importantly, more of the over-fifty population will choose to stay working for long as they can.

All past and recent data from governmental, educational, and
corporate sources indicate boomers' desire to stay working pro-
ductively into and through their retirement. Work is remunerative, healthy, enjoyable, and stimulating.

Over the next several years, there will be more national acceptance of older workers. Trends suggest that there will be older workers in all aspects of the work force, from supermarket clerks to physicians.

Income generation will remain the number-one driver to stay on the job or, more probably, to seek new work. But within the many levels of income need, many people will do work they enjoy. Some percentage who do not need any supplemental income will find the chance to do the job or avocation of their dreams.

The rise in the number of retirees looking for new work will lead to corresponding increases in products and services to assist them in the pursuit of new and different jobs. As older-worker-oriented employment proliferates, there will be a parallel rise in placement agencies dedicated to finding work for older job seekers, more career coaches specializing in motivating this age group, and more seminars, books, and pamphlets providing helpful hints about what kind of work to do in later years.

The Mega Community: An Imagined Place

A few miles south from the center of Myrtle Beach, South Carolina, is New Way City, a mammoth residential compound, the latest idea in intergenerational living. Its main building is a forty-story skyscraper.

The central idea was to build a habitat where old and young could live and mingle together. Most of the full-time staff are under fifty, attracted by the guarantee of good-paying jobs and continuing employment. Portions of each job class were also allocated to the older workers who could partner with others to do part-time work or arrange flexible work schedules as they aged.

The complex has food courts, movie theaters, supermarkets and shops, swimming pools, day-care centers, and a gym and spa all contained within it. Fully staffed medical facilities, dentists' office, therapy rooms, dialysis centers, and other health-related necessities for older residents are located in an adjacent wing, an elevator ride and a short walk from the main building.

The University of South Carolina opened Eastern Beach Community College, offering adult education and other courses to accommodate the 25,000 new inhabitants.

Sherry and Hank Joyce, both fifty-eight, from Lima, Ohio, opted for early retirement and decided on New Way City because it offered them continuing work opportunities, an age mixture of residents, and excellent tennis and beach facilities. They became members of an affordable HMO group for workers run by the complex, an indispensable boon since Medicare was seven years away.

Sherry can continue doing financial planning and tax returns for people within the complex. She's on the waiting list to become an adjunct professor in accounting at Eastern Beach Community College. Hank has switched occupations from machine shop foreman to Web design, thanks to new graphic skills acquired through night courses at a branch of Ohio State University in Lima.

The Joyces were also impressed by New Way City's carefully thought-out health-care facilities, designed to service an aging population. Older residents can choose to install built-in computerized medical modules that monitor different health diagnostics daily. The information is automatically transported into the complex's medical data banks where computers immediately flag any dramatic or sudden changes in blood pressure, heartbeat, and other medical conditions. In an emergency, trained medical staff is minutes away.

The Joyces are avid tennis fans and envision a rotation of leisure and work throughout the sunny South Carolina seasons. New Way City offers full tennis court facilities including clay and hard surfaces, night lights for evening play, and a variety of singles and doubles leagues. Both Joyces have volunteered to teach youth and high school tennis.

Sherry expressed the same sentiments that others her age have voiced. "Basically, we're reinventing ourselves in ways that the age group before us never considered. We refer to these 'Children of the Fifties' as the Silent Generation because they were content to stay with the status quo and not rock the boat. This was true for retirement where they headed south to live permanently, enjoy the sun, and become involved in their own communities that were composed mainly of other retirees the same age.

"We boomers, on the other hand, are a 'Let's change things for the better' generation. We see the benefit of mixed age and mixed usage communities. Our attitudes toward well-being—physical and spiritual—also differ. We are concerned, maybe 'obsessed' is the right word, with fitness.

"Maybe at one time we were concerned only with ourselves, making money, keeping up with the Joneses, the 'Me' Generation. But over time we've changed for the better and have developed a more altruistic attitude toward the outside world, especially the environment."

New Way City has numerous coordinated volunteer programs to provide service workers to some of the elderly and infirm within the complex. It also seeks out nannies to assist in the day-care center for working parents. Residents access the volunteer assignments online or stop by at the Volunteer Office in the main floor of the compound.

As some of the older residents die, their surviving spouses have the option of moving to smaller quarters at lower monthly costs. One block is entirely assisted living, which also uses many volunteers within the community.

New Way City has become the bellwether for intergenerational communal residences in the United States.

Final Predictions

These are some educated guesses about what work and retirement will look like in the future.

1. The ongoing trend in the United States has been toward a service-oriented society. Predictions are that by 2010, more than 85 percent of all jobs will fit into this category. The economy will seek brainpower over physical power with the result that the hard-labor segment will continue to decrease. In the

future there will be fewer blue-collar jobs for seniors. Retrain soon or you will lose out on these positions.

2. A bigger senior customer base will create a demand for more senior service people in all areas of businesses but especially in retail. Retailers will seek out older workers who can relate to the aging population of shoppers.

3. Community colleges will experience a windfall of new applicants, many of them retired or soon-to-be-retired people. Business and technical courses will see more students in the over-fifty group than before. Seniors will also teach these courses as adjunct professors, incorporating their life and business experiences into the classwork.

4. There will also be extended groups of professional caregivers, many of whom will be immigrants (legal or not). Foreign countries will start to offer care services at costs less than in the United States.

5. Many people fifty and older will become investment experts. They will seek out investment research and reading material and make constant investment decisions. Some may become day traders, spending hours on the Internet.

6. Some investment advisers forecast that the retiring baby boomers will no longer put money into stock equities but will pull income out for living expenses. How big a drain will this be on the stock market? Time will tell.

* * *

A Final Note

In the past, there were three stages of life: childhood/education, work, and retirement. Now there are four stages: childhood/education, working, retirement, and ReWorking. We want everyone to enjoy work in all its forms. As the English poet Shelley wrote, "Grow old along with me. The best is yet to be."

Appendix: Resources

Following is a list of Web sites, addresses, and telephone numbers of useful sources to find information for governmental information at federal and state levels.

Social Security Administration
Office of Public Inquiries
Windsor Park Building
6401 Security Boulevard
Baltimore, MD 21235
800-772-1213 (twenty-four-hour phone service)
www.socialsecurity.gov
also *www.ssa.gov*
and *www.medicare.gov*

U.S. Department of Labor
Frances Perkins Building
200 Constitution Avenue, N.W.
Washington, DC 20210
866-4-USA-DOL
www.dol.gov

U.S. Bureau of Labor Statistics
Postal Square Building
2 Massachusetts Avenue, N.E.
Washington, DC 20212-0001
Phone: 202-691-5200
www.bls.gov

Internal Revenue Service
800-829-1040
www.IRS.gov

State Departments of Labor
The best place to look for jobs locally is to contact your state's department of labor. On the Web sites are often job placement possibilities. If you have questions about work for seniors or new programs designed for older workers, the state labor department should be your first contact.

Alabama
Department of Labor
P.O. Box 303500
Montgomery, AL 36130-3500
Phone: 334-242-3460
Fax: 334-240-3417
www.dir.state.al.us

Alaska
Department of Labor
P.O. Box 21149
Juneau, AK 99801-1149
Phone: 907-465-2700
Fax: 907-465-2784
www.labor.state.ak.us

Arizona
State Labor Department
P.O. Box 19070
Phoenix, AZ 85005-9070
Phone: 602-542-4515
Fax: 602-542-8097
www.ica.state.az.us

Arkansas
Department of Labor
10421 W. Markham
Little Rock, AR 72205
Phone: 501-682-4541
Fax: 501-682-4535
www.state.ar.us/labor

California
Division of Labor
455 Golden Gate Avenue
San Francisco, CA 94102
Phone: 415-703-4810
Fax: 415-703-4807
www.dir.ca.gov

Colorado
Department of Labor and
Employment
633 17th Street
Denver, CO 80202-3660
Phone: 303-318-8000
Fax: 330-318-8048
www.coworkforce.com

Connecticut
Labor Department
200 Folly Brook Boulevard
Wethersfield, CT 06109-1114
Phone: 860-263-6505
Fax: 860-263-6529
www.ctdol.state.ct.us

Delaware
Department of Labor
4425 N. Market Street
Wilmington, DE 19802
Phone: 302-761-8000
Fax: 302-761-6621
www.delawareworks.com

District of Columbia

Department of Employment
Services
54 New York Avenue
Washington, DC 20002
Phone: 202-671-1900
Fax: 202-673-6993
www.does.ci.washington.dc.us

Florida

Agency for Workforce
Innovation
Caldwell Building
107 East Madison Street
Tallahassee, FL 32399-4120
Phone: 850-245-7105
Fax: 850-921-3223
www.floridajobs.org

Georgia

Department of Labor
148 International Boulevard,
N.E.
Atlanta, GA 30303
Phone: 404-656-3011
Fax: 404-656-2683
www.dol.state.ga.us

Hawaii

Department of Labor
830 Punchbowl Street
Honolulu, HI 96813
Phone: 808-586-8865/8844
Fax: 808-586-9099
www.hawaii.gov/labor

Idaho

Department of Labor
317 W. Main Street
Boise, ID 83735-0001
Phone: 208-332-3579
Fax: 208-334-6430
www.labor.state.id.us

Illinois

Department of Labor
160 N. LaSalle Street
Chicago, IL 60601
Phone: 312-793-1808
Fax: 312-793-5257
www.state.il.us/agency/idol

Indiana

Department of Labor
Indiana Government Center
South
402 W. Washington Street
Indianapolis, IN 46204-2739
Phone: 317-232-2378
Fax: 317-233-5381
www.state.in.us/labor

Iowa

Iowa Workforce Development
1000 E. Grand Avenue
Des Moines, IA 50319-0209
Phone: 515-281-5365
Fax: 515-281-4698
www.iowaworkforce.org/labor

Kansas

Department of Human
Resources
401 S.W. Topeka Boulevard
Topeka, KS 66603-3182
Phone: 785-296-7474
Fax: 785-368-6294
www.dol.ks.gov

Kentucky

Department of Labor
1047 U.S. Highway 127
Frankfort, KY 40601-4381
Phone: 502-564-3070
Fax: 502-564-5387
www.labor.ky.gov

Louisiana

Department of Labor
P.O. Box 94094
Baton Rouge, LA 70804-9094
Phone: 225-342-3011
Fax: 225-342-3778
www.ldol.state.la.us

Maine

Department of Labor
19 Union Street
P.O. Box 259
Augusta, ME 04332-0259
Phone: 207-287-3787
Fax: 207-287-5292
www.maine.gov/labor

Maryland

Department of Labor
1100 Eutaw Street
Baltimore, MD 21201
Phone: 410-767-2999
Fax: 410-767-2986
www.dllr.state.md.us

Massachusetts

Department of Labor
1 Ashburton Place
Boston, MA 02108
Phone: 617-727-6573
Fax: 617-727-1090
www.mass.gov/dol

Michigan

Department of Labor
P.O. Box 30004
Lansing, MI 48909
Phone: 517-373-3034
Fax: 517-373-2129
www.michigan.gov/cis

Minnesota

Department of Labor and
Industry
443 Lafayette Road
St. Paul, MN 55155
Phone: 651-284-5010
Fax: 651-284-5721
www.doli.state.mn.us

Mississippi

Department of Employment
P.O. Box 1699
Jackson, MS 39215-1699
Phone: 601-321-6100
Fax: 601-321-6104
www.mdes.ms.gov

Missouri

Department of Labor
P.O. Box 504
Jefferson City, MO
65102-0504
Phone: 573-751-9691
Fax: 573-751-4135
www.dolir.mo.gov

Montana

Department of Labor
P.O. Box 1728
Helena, MT 59624-1728
Phone: 406-444-9091
Fax: 406-444-1394
www.dli.mt.gov

Nebraska

Department of Labor
550 S. 16th Street
Lincoln, NE 68509-4600
Phone: 402-471-3405
Fax: 402-471-2318
www.dol.state.ne.us

Nevada

Department of Business and
Industry
555 E. Washington Avenue
Las Vegas, NV 89101-1050
Phone: 702-486-2650
Fax: 702-486-2660
www.laborcommissioner.com

New Hampshire

Department of Labor
95 Pleasant Street
Concord, NH 03301
Phone: 603-271-3171
Fax: 603-271-6852
www.labor.state.nh.us

New Jersey

Department of Labor
John Fitch Plaza
Trenton, NJ 08625-0110
Phone: 609-292-2323
Fax: 609-633-9271
www.state.nj.us/labor

New Mexico

Department of Labor
401 Broadway, N.E.
Albuquerque, NM
87103-1928
Phone: 505-841-8409
Fax: 505-841-8491
www.dws.state.nm.us

New York
Department of Labor
State Campus Building
Albany, NY 12240-0003
Phone: 518-457-2741
Fax: 518-457-6908
www.labor.state.ny.us

North Carolina
Department of Labor
4 W. Edenton Street
Raleigh, NC 27601-1092
Phone: 919-733-0359
Fax: 919-733-0223
www.nclabor.com

North Dakota
Department of Labor
State Capitol Building
600 East Boulevard Avenue
Department 406
Bismarck, ND 58505-0340
Phone: 701-328-2660
Fax: 701-328-2031
www.state.nd.us/labor

Ohio
Ohio Department of Job &
Family Services
4300 Kimberly Parkway
Columbus, Ohio 43232
Phone: 614-995-7066
Fax: 614-466-6873
www.jfs.ohio.gov

Oklahoma
Department of Labor
4001 N. Lincoln Boulevard
Oklahoma City, OK
73105-5212
Phone: 405-528-1500,
ext. 200
Fax: 405-528-5751
www.state.ok.us/~okdol

Oregon
Bureau of Labor and Industries
800 N.E. Oregon Street,
Suite 32
Portland, OR 97232
Phone: 503-731-4070
Fax: 503-731-4103
www.boli.state.or.us

Pennsylvania
Department of Labor and
Industry
1700 Labor and Industry
Building
Harrisburg, PA 17120
Phone: 717-787-5279
Fax: 717-787-8826
www.dli.state.pa.us

Puerto Rico

Department of Labor
Edificio Prudencio Rivera
Martinez
505 Munoz Rivera Avenue
G.P.O. Box 3088
Hato Rey, PR 00918
Phone: 787-754-2119 or 2120
Fax: 787-753-9550
*www.dol.gov/dol/location
.htm#PR*

Rhode Island

Department of Labor and
Training
1511 Pontiac Avenue
Cranston, RI 02920
Phone: 401-462-8870
Fax: 401-462-8872
www.dlt.state.ri.us

South Carolina

Department of Labor
110 Center View Drive
P.O. Box 11329
Columbia, SC 29211-1329
Phone: 803-896-4300
Fax: 803-896-4393
www.llr.state.sc.us

South Dakota

Department of Labor
700 Governors Drive
Pierre, SD 57501-2291
Phone: 605-773-3101
Fax: 605-773-4211
www.state.sd.us/dol/dol.htm

Tennessee

Department of Labor
710 James Robertson Parkway
Nashville, TN 37243-0655
Phone: 615-741-6642
Fax: 615-741-5078
www.state.tn.us/labor-wfd

Texas

Texas Workforce Commission
101 E. 15th Street
Austin, TX 78778
Phone: 512-463-0735
Fax: 512-475-2321
www.twc.state.tx.us

Utah

Labor Commission
P.O. Box 146610
Salt Lake City, UT
84114-6610
Phone: 801-530-6880
Fax: 801-530-6804
www.laborcommission.utah.gov

Vermont
Department of Labor
5 Green Mountain Drive
P.O. Box 488
Montpelier, VT 05602-0488
Phone: 802-828-4000
Fax: 802-828-4022
www.labor.vermont.gov

Virginia
Department of Labor and
Industry
13 S. 13th Street
Richmond, VA 23219
Phone: 804-786-2377
Fax: 804-371-6524
www.dli.state.va.us

Washington
Department of Labor
P.O. Box 44001
Olympia, WA 98504-4001
Phone: 360-902-4203
Fax: 360-902-4202
www.lni.wa.gov

West Virginia
Division of Labor
State Capitol Complex
Charleston, WV 25305
Phone: 304-558-7890
Fax: 304-558-3797
www.wvlabor.org

Wisconsin
Department of Workforce
Development
201 E. Washington Avenue
Madison, WI 53707-7946
Phone: 608-267-9692
Fax: 608-266-1784
www.dwd.state.wi.us

Wyoming
Department of Employment
1510 E. Pershing Boulevard
Cheyenne, WY 82002
Phone: 307-777-7672
Fax: 307-777-5805
http://wydoe.state.wy.us

Index

About the Authors

ALLYN FREEMAN has been writing professionally for more than thirty years with credits in television, including *M*A*S*H* and *Hart to Hart*. He has written, coauthored, ghosted, and contributed to eleven books, including *The Leadership Genius of Alfred P. Sloan, CEO of General Motors* and recently *The Campbell Apartment—Cocktails from Another Era*. He was the featured speaker at the New York Conference Board's New Marketing Ideas Seminar. He is a graduate of Brown University, the Thunderbird Institute of International Trade, and Columbia University Business School.

BOB GORMAN has had a successful thirty-five-year career in entrepreneurial financial planning and as an insurance executive. He has served in senior managerial positions for many well-known U.S. insurance companies; in addition, he was the general manager of many Philadelphia-based regional branch agencies. He has been the recipient of numerous sales and managerial company awards for outstanding performance. He is certified in Financial Planning and Estate Planning. He is a graduate of Brown University, Iona College Business School, and the College for Financial Planning.

www.ReWorkingRetirement.com